Kitchen Artworks

Fruits and Vegetable carving book

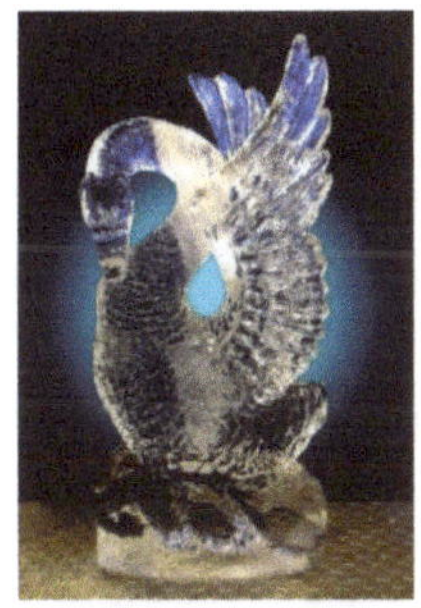
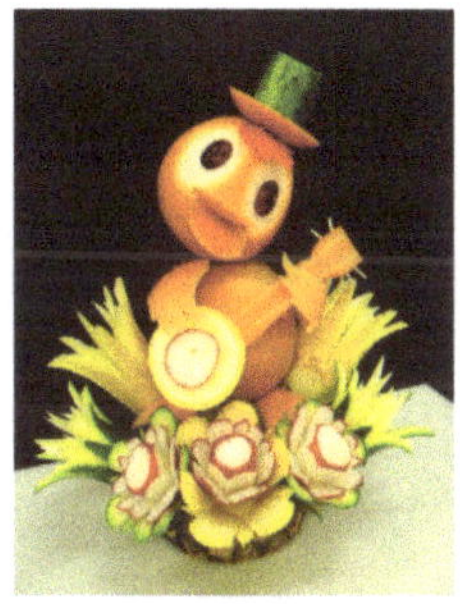
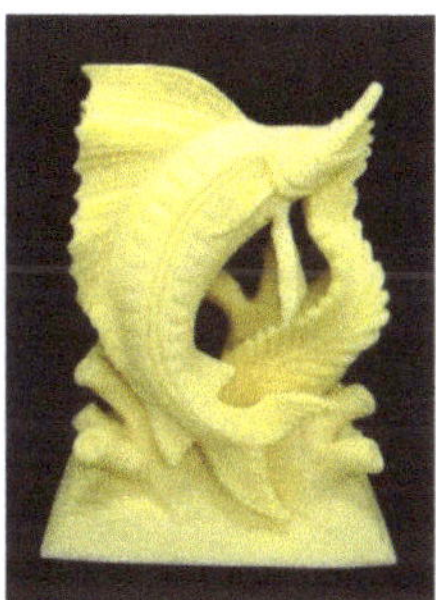
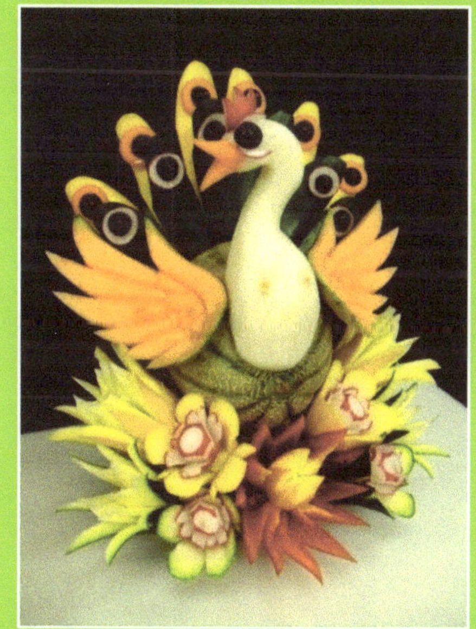
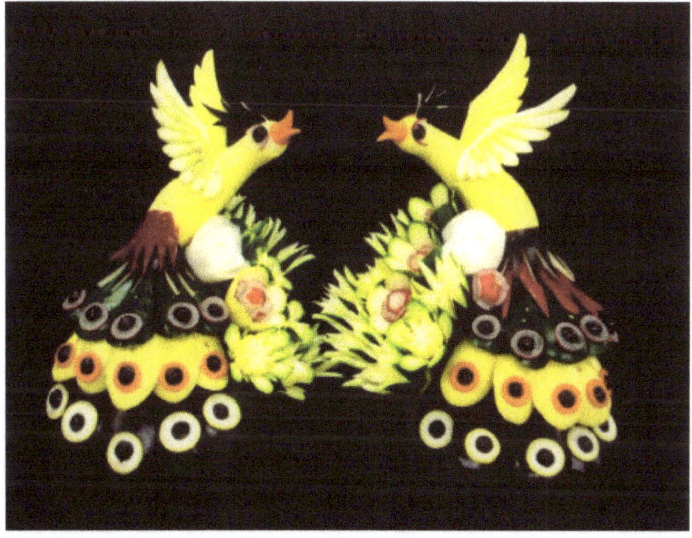

Basic Instructional Book of Carving
Step-By-Step Guide and Technique, with
Watermelon Carving, Ice sculpture and
Tallow-wax butter Sculpture

Kitchen Artworks

Fruits and Vegetable carving book

Culinary kitchen artist and ideas by:

Rizalde Gagaring
and
Albert Pajanonot

Gotham Books

30 N Gould St.
Ste. 20820, Sheridan, WY 82801
https://gothambooksinc.com/

Phone: 1 (307) 464-7800

Published by Gotham Books (August 1, 2024)

ISBN: 979-8-3303-1421-8 (P)
ISBN: 979-8-3303-1422-5 (E)

Because of the dynamic nature of the Internet, any web addresses or links contained in this book may have changed since publication and may no longer be valid.

The views expressed in this work are solely those of the author and do not necessarily reflect the views of the publisher, and the publisher hereby disclaims any responsibility for them.

Dedication

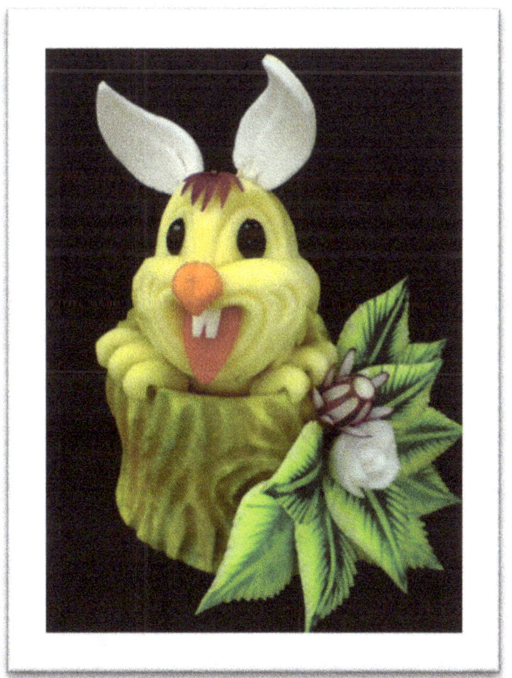

To all the chefs around the world.

This book, The Kitchen Artworks – Fruit and Vegetable Carving Book,

is dedicated to all of you.

Acknowledgements

My gratitude and special thanks to all our previous companies, Carnival Cruise Line, Celebrity Cruise Line, Norwegian Cruise Line, Star Cruises and the most famous ocean liner in the world Queen Mary 2.

We are proud to have been a part of the inaugural team of Queen Elizabeth, the new ship of Cunard Line 2010.

I would like to thank my colleague Arnel Bagayana and Orlando Aseoche who helping me to become realty our vision and share this to some who want to learn this magical talent.

Foreword

This book is intended to be a Basic Instructional Book of Carving showing the step-by-step guide of its techniques and methods.

The highly detailed photographs in this practical manual illustrate the basic techniques in fruit and vegetable animation for the creation of centerpiece and culinary decoration for all occasions.

This book may be used as a guide in creating displays to be used in various functions and special occasions like weddings, birthdays, anniversaries, Christmas Gala Buffets, New Year's Midnight Extravaganza Buffets and Thanksgiving dinners. It is also an excellent reference material for self-study purposes as well as a highly detailed and practical textbook during the formal study of Culinary Art courses.

We are sure that the culinary students and readers of this book will appreciate the unique and modern techniques of this kitchen artist.

I extend my deepest gratitude to the one who provides this artistic talent, the Creator of this beautiful world and the Giver of our life.

ALPAJ

About my co-author

Chef Rizalde Gagaring was born in Paete, Laguna, Philippines. He first started to develop his sculpting talent in wood, fruit and vegetable and ice carving at the age of 15. Later on, he focused on improving his own techniques and ideas.

He creates fabulous fruit and vegetable carving masterpieces and this outstanding skill of his allows him to also produce beautiful works of art using ice blocks, tallow-wax butter and Styrofoam.

He has been working in the culinary field for the past 20 years on board many different luxury cruise liners. In 2010, he was proclaimed winner in the Chef Salon Culinary Cooking Competition in the Fruit and Vegetable carving category.

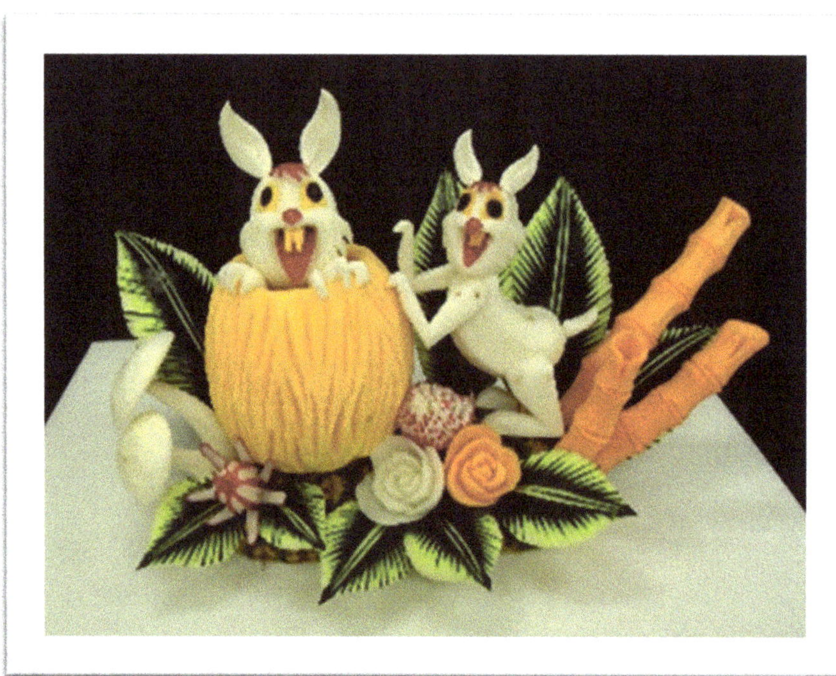

Message

Finally, we are presenting this carving book which provides step-by-step guides and techniques for culinary kitchen art decorations and centrepieces.

We can say this is a different book as compared to other books on kitchen art decoration and garnishing. It presents various sculptures combined with decoration varieties making use of different materials. We guarantee you will be satisfied with this book.

Together with all those we have extended our appreciation to; we proudly present to you "Kitchen Artworks" – a book you are going to love.

AlPAJ

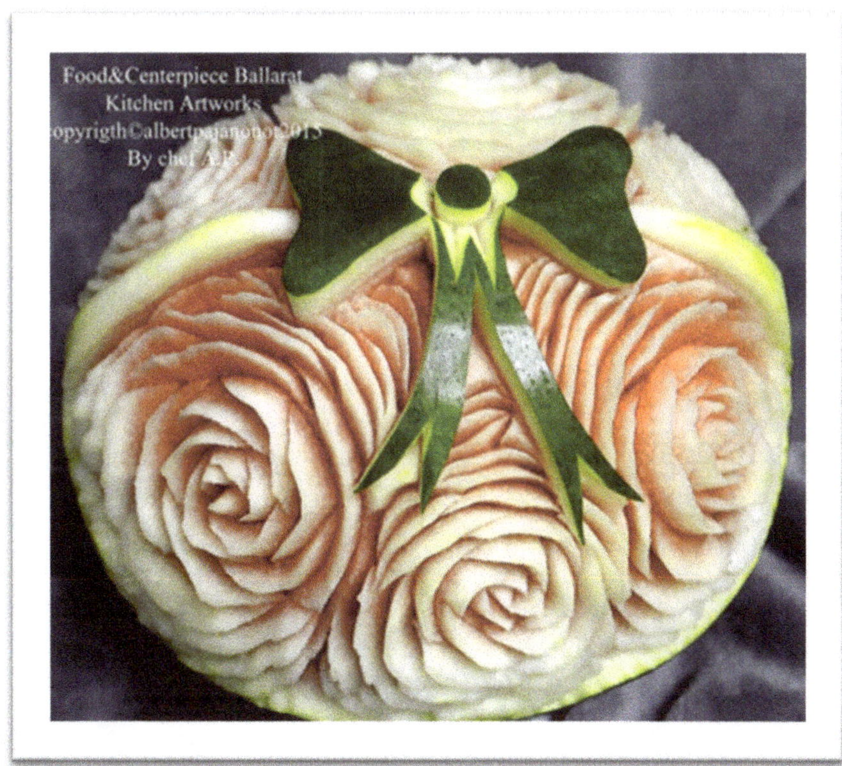

Table of Content

Fruits and Vegetable Carving

About Fruits and Vegetable Carving

This is for everyone, from beginners to those in the advanced level. This enables one to acquire the skill needed to be able to translate ideas into the knowledgeable form and the skill to engrave.

The Fruits and Vegetable Carving have been adopted all over the world. Asian food artists in China, Japan, Philippines, Korea, India, Vietnam, Indonesia and Thailand consider the fruits and vegetable carving as part of the presentation of every meal. The stunning designs are used as the center of attraction of the overall food decoration.

Technique and Method

Pointed Knife - a very unique instrument having a particular form, a flexible blade and is very sharp and pointed.

Technique - hold the knife like you would a pen. Use your finger to balance your hand then start to engrave. Remember to always cut from left to right about the length of your finger. Keep your mind focused on what you are doing.

Sculpture

This is the art of creating a three-dimensional work of art through carving, engraving, constructing work and modelling and casting making use of various materials like ice, whole fruits, Styrofoam, wood, stone and clay.

Carving – the object or design formed after shaping and cutting various materials such as fruits and vegetables, a huge ice block, tallow-wax butter and chocolate modelling paste.

Modelling – a copy of an object made on a smaller scale of the original.

Casting – making objects with the use of moulds.

Three-Dimensional – a work of act with three dimensions either created through sculpting or any other work method.

Things to Remember in Fruits and Vegetable Carving

It is highly recommended that constant practice is needed to achieve perfection. Patience is a must. Be extra careful when carving for the first time. Knowledge of the correct proportions is important. Lastly, have a pointed and sharp paring knife and other carving tools on hand as these will be of help to you.

Turkey

This figure is completely made out of fruits and vegetables. A whole cantaloupe is used for the body while a pineapple is for the base.

This is a good center piece for a cold cuts mirror, or as a buffet line decoration or for other different kinds of occasions like a thanksgiving party, a ploughman buffet set-up or even for a kid's party.

Fruits, Vegetables and Materials Needed:

1 pc white radish, 2 whole cantaloupes, 1 pc bell pepper, 1 pc carrot, 1 whole pineapple, 8 pcs zucchini, 6 pcs squash, 4 pcs red radish and 7 pcs grapes.

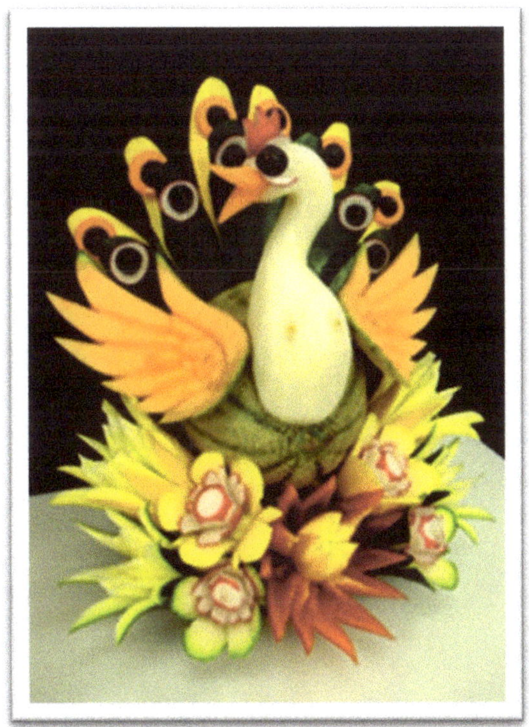

Methods and Instructions:

Figure 1.1 to 1.5	–	To make the neck and the head of the turkey
Figure 2.1 to 2.5	–	To make the beak
Figure 3.1 to 3.3	–	To make the body of the character
Figure 4.1 to 4.5	–	To make the eyeballs and the crown of the turkey
Figure 5.1 to 5.12	–	To make the tail of the turkey
Figure 6.1 to 6.4	–	To make the wings of the turkey
Figure 7.1 to 7.5	–	To connect the base and the vegetable flower

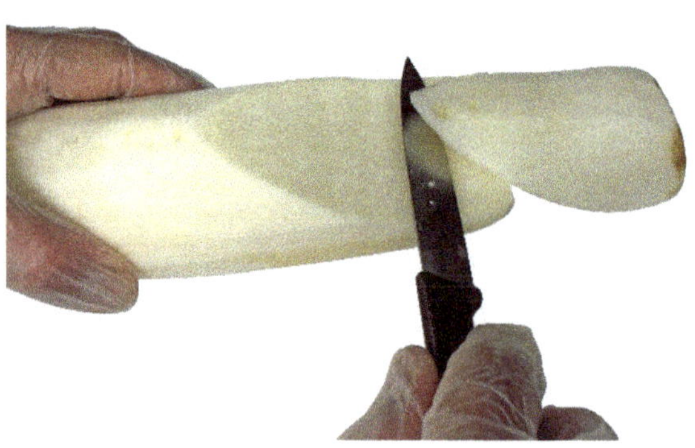

Figure 1.1 – In a slanting position, cut both sides of the white radish.

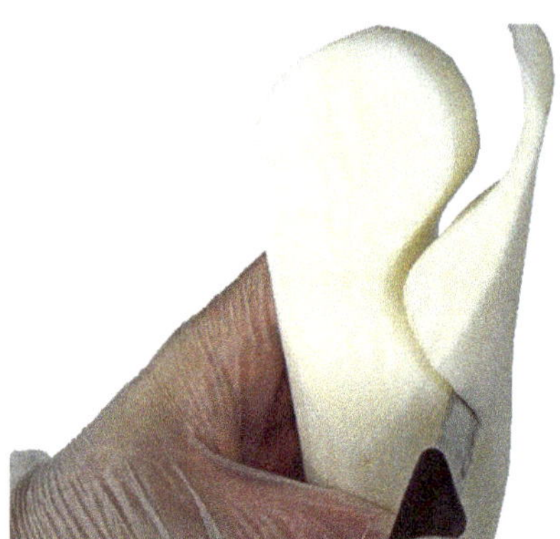

Figure 1.2 – Starting from the tip of the right side, slide the paring knife downward is a letter S motion. This is the back part of the turkey.

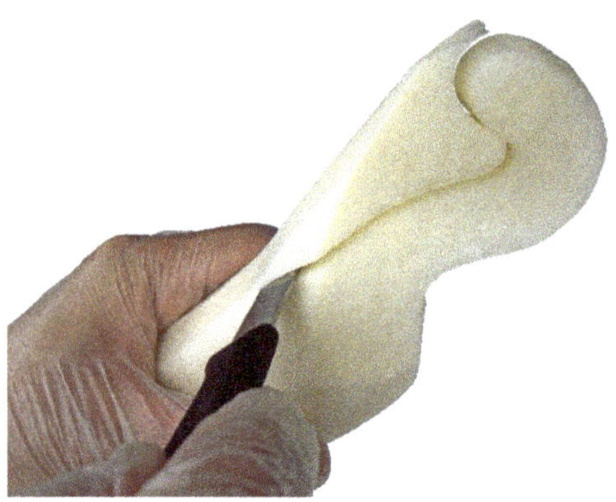

Figure 1.3 – Hold the radish and make a deep cut to shape the neck by moving the paring knife in a number 7 motion all the way down the body of the radish.

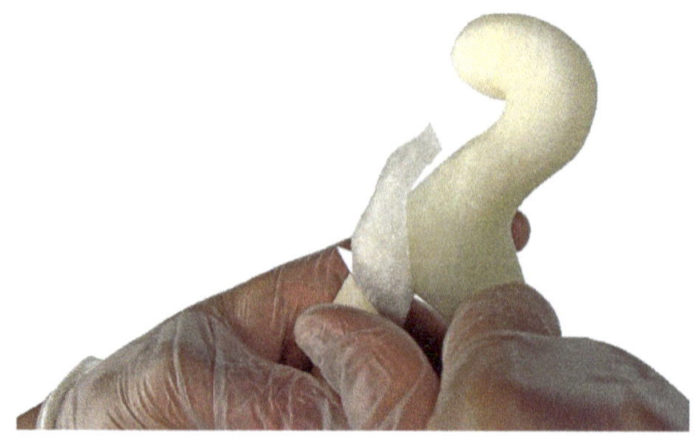

Figure 1.4 – Clean-up the entire corner and rough portions around the radish.

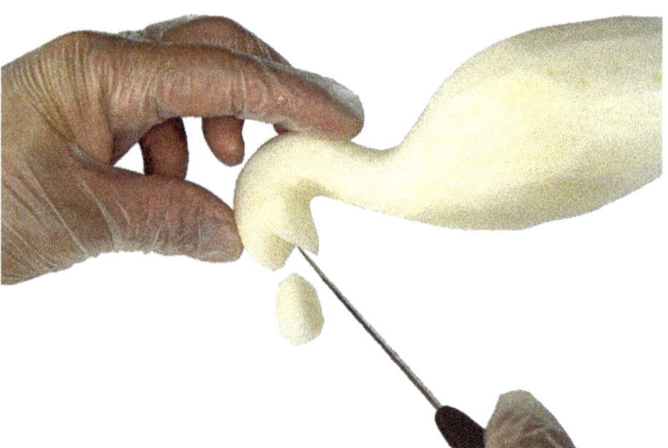

Figure 1.5 – Make a v-shaped cut into the head.

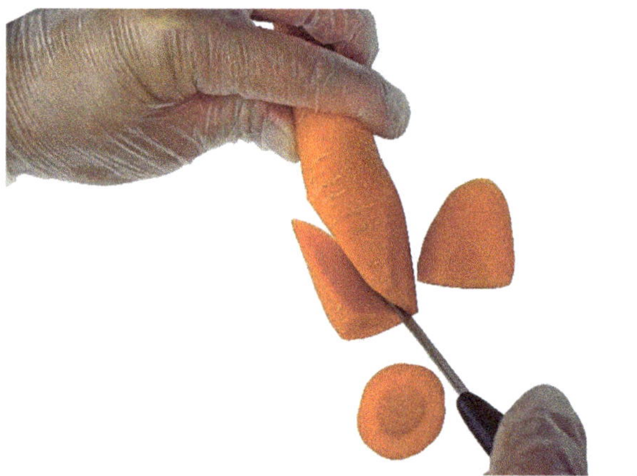

Figure 2.1 – Cut the carrot on both sides to make a v-shape cut.

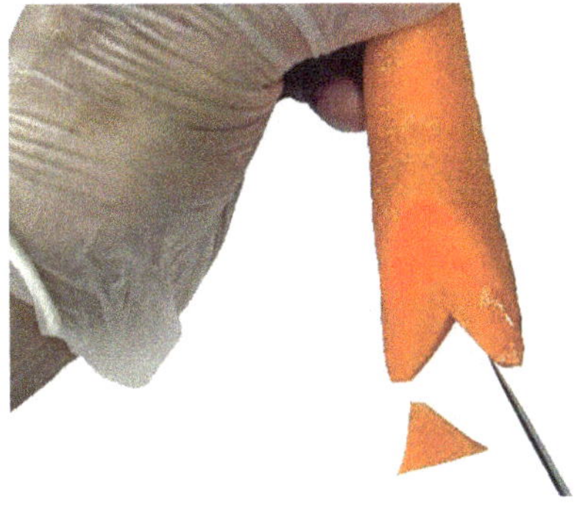

Figure 2.2 – Turn the carrot and make another v-shape cut again.

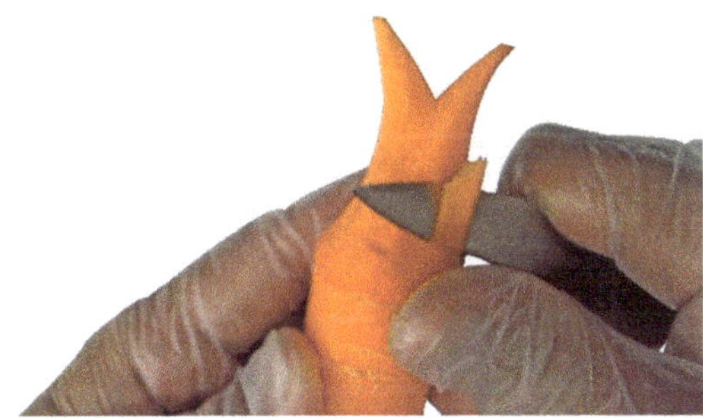

Figure 2.3 – Clean up and shape the beak.

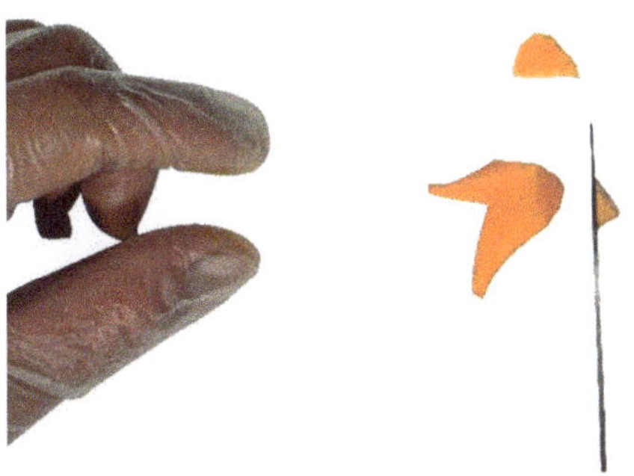

Figure 2.4 – Cut a v- shape on the base of the beak.

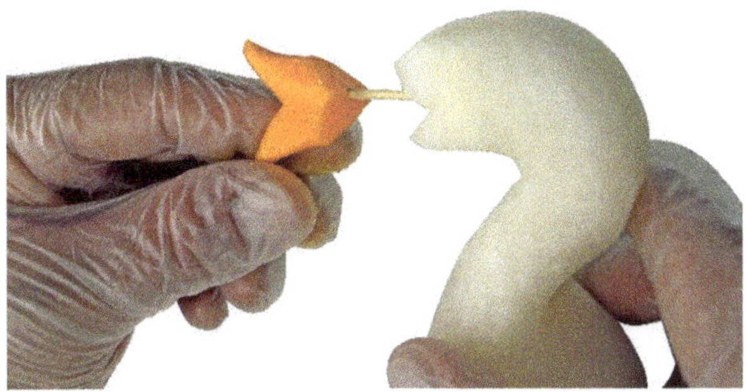

Figure 2.5 – Attach the beak using a toothpick.

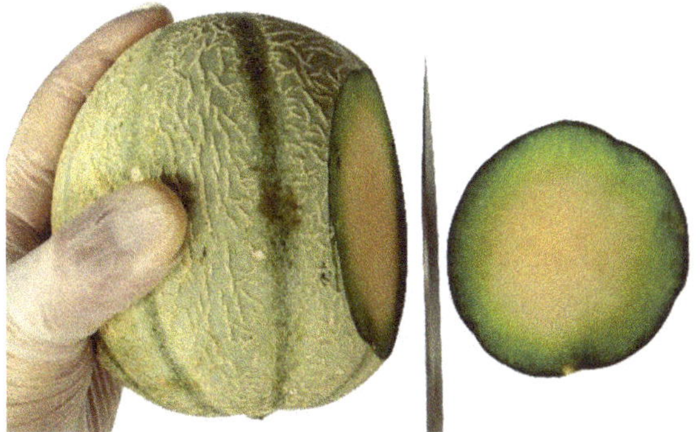

Figure 3.1 – Get the cantaloupe and cut away a portion of its side which will form part of the body of the turkey.

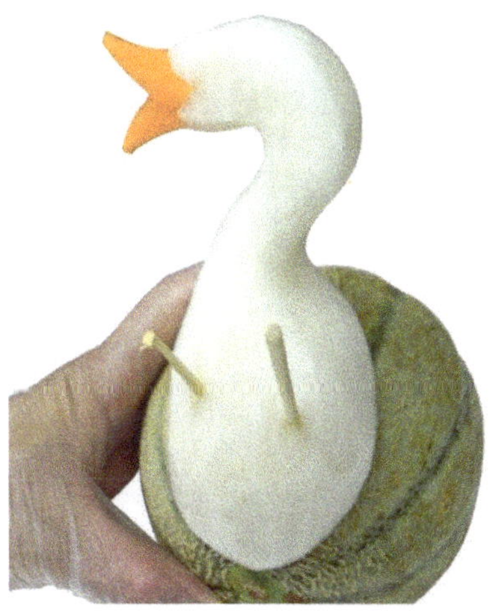

Figure 3.2 – Attach the radish to the cut-away portion of the cantaloupe using bamboo skewers.

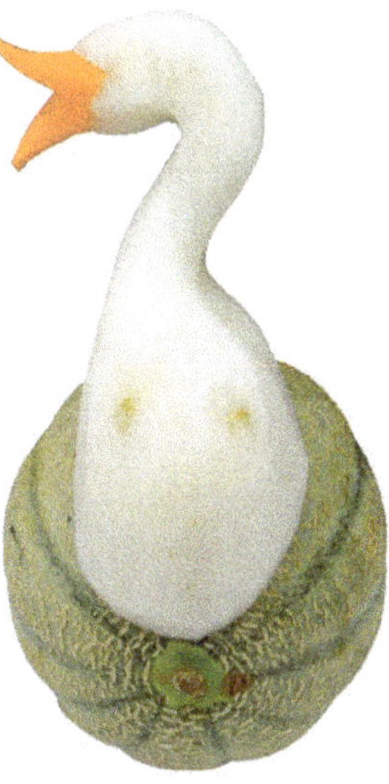

Figure 3.3 – The figure now shows proportions of the Turkey's whole body.

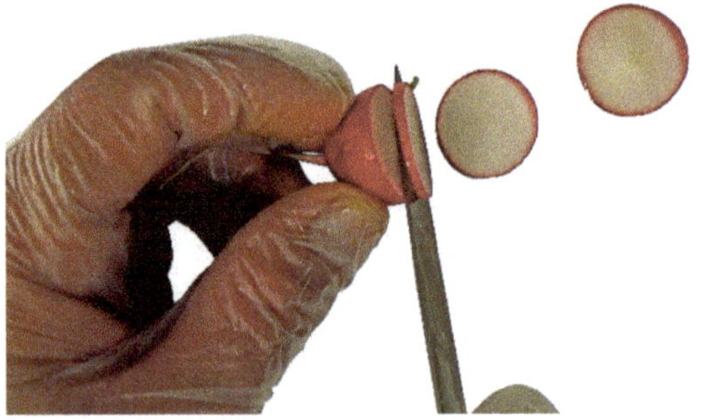

Figure 4.1 – For the shadows of the eyes, thinly slice one red radish.

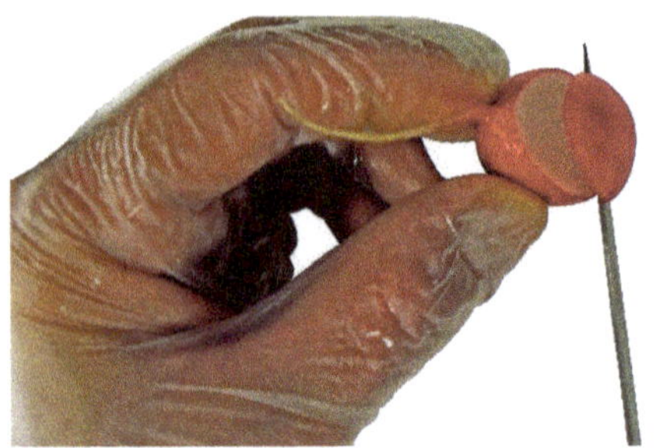

Figure 4.2 – For the crown of the turkey, cut one side of another red radish.

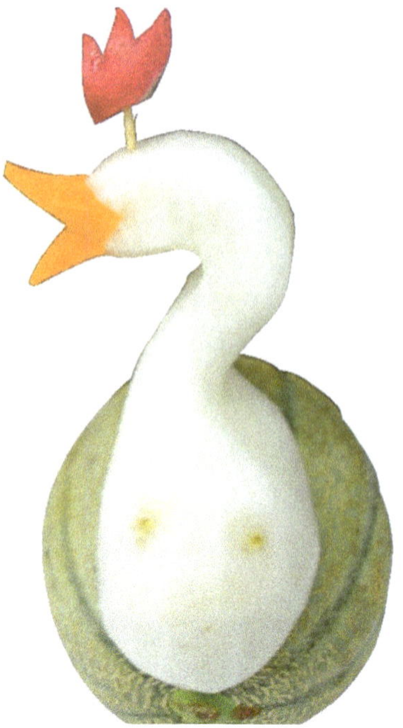

Figure 4.4 – Attach the crown to the head of the turkey using a toothpick.

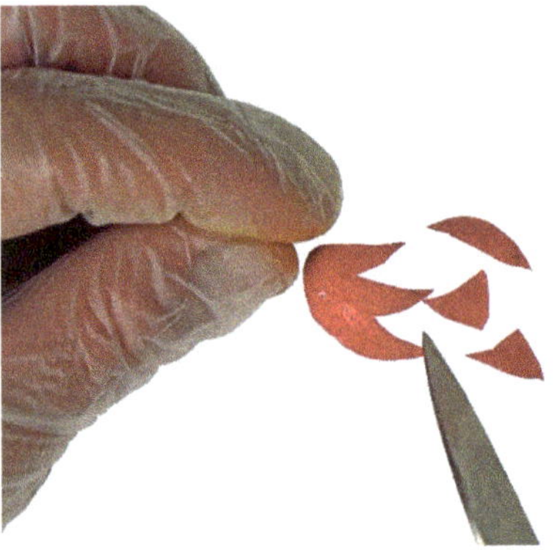

Figure 4.3 – Cut in the v- shapes to form the crown for the head of the turkey.

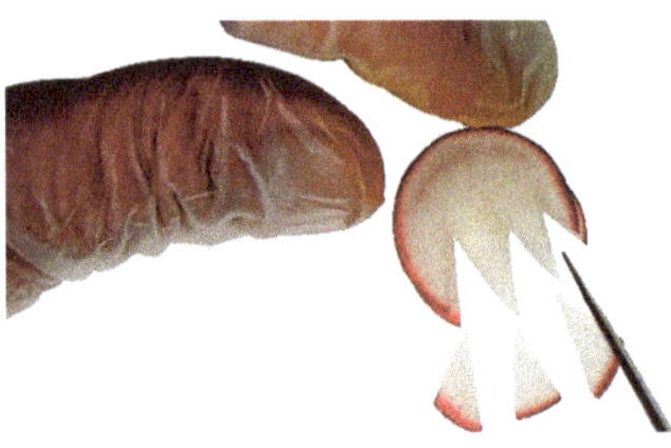

Figure 4.5 – Using the thin slices of red radish (Figure 4.1), cut in triangular shapes as shown in the picture.

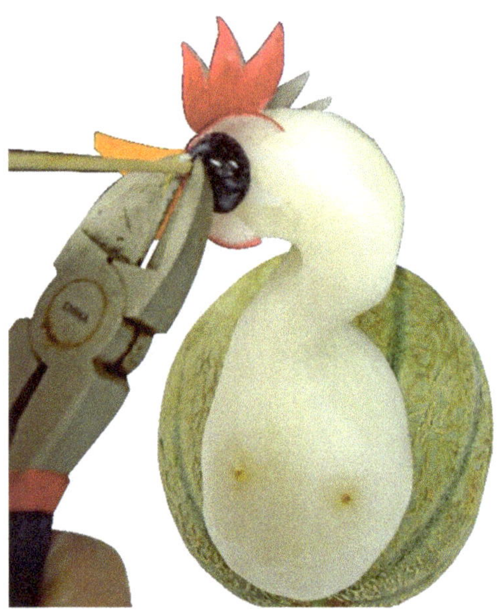

Figure 4.6 – Cut small portions of the grapes for the eye balls then together with the eye shadows (Figure 4.5), connect to the head of the turkey using a toothpick.

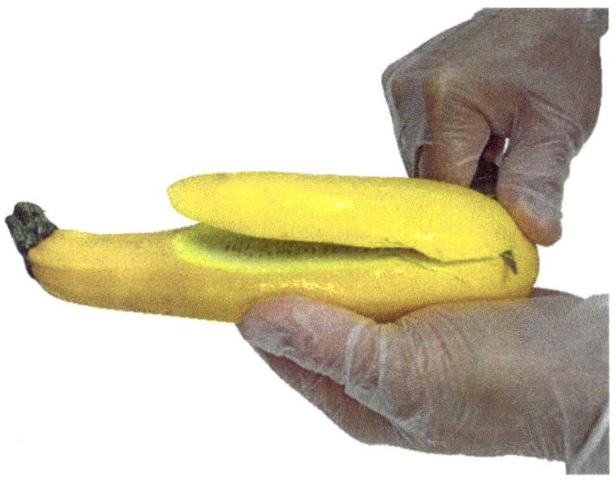

Figure 5.1 – Cut the outer side of the yellow squash into slices of 4 to 5 inches in length.

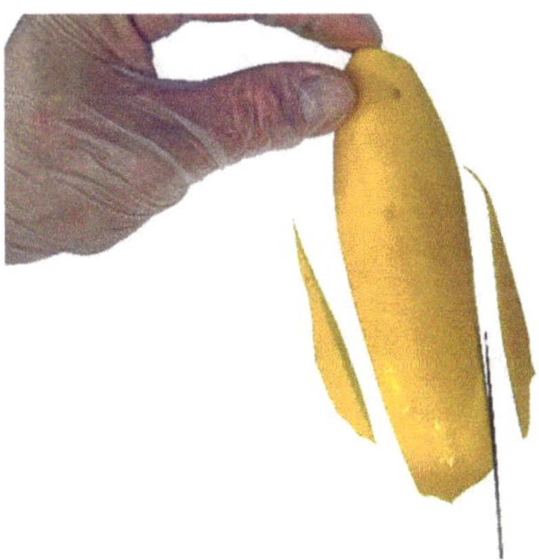

Figure 5.2 – Cut away the side parts of each slice.

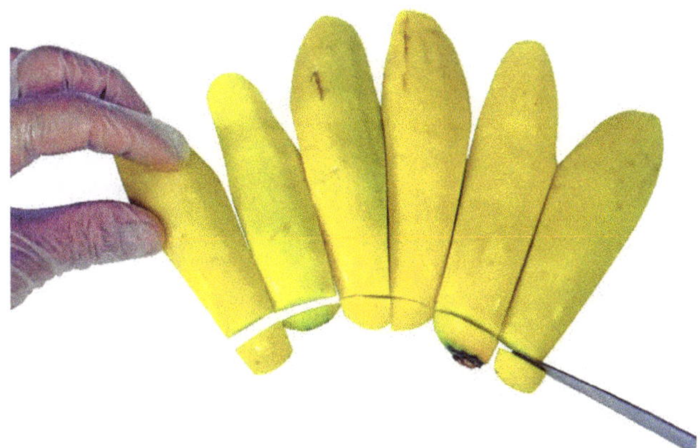

Figure 5.3 – Assemble together the first layer of the tail as shown in the picture. Cut a portion of the lower part to make connection to the body of the turkey easier.

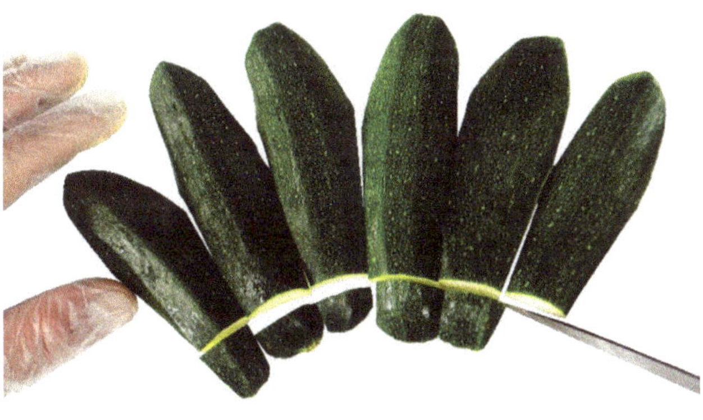

Figure 5.4 – Do the same procedure with the zucchini to make the second layer of the tail. Take note that the second layer must be shorter than the first layer.

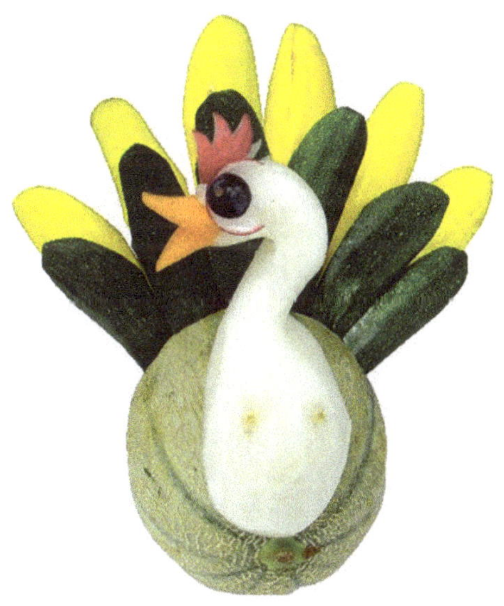

Figure 5.5 – Attach the first layer of the tail to the cantaloupe by using bamboo skewers.

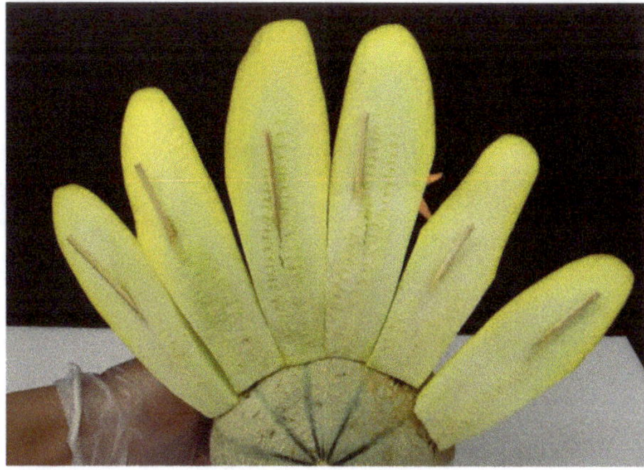

Figure 5.6 – The picture shows the correct procedure and technique in assembling the 1st layer of the tail.

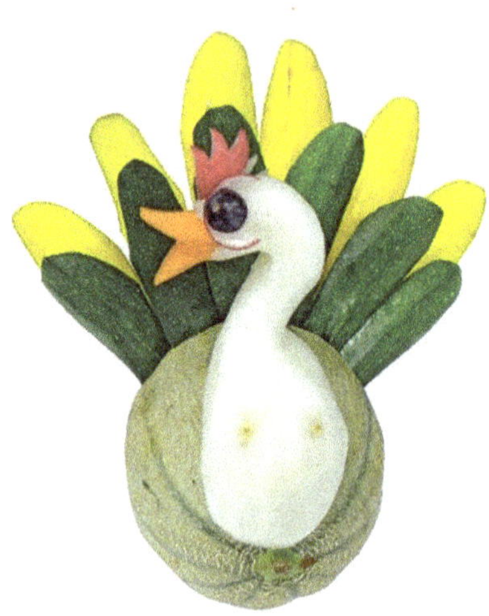

Figure 5.7 – Attach the second layer using the same procedure and technique.

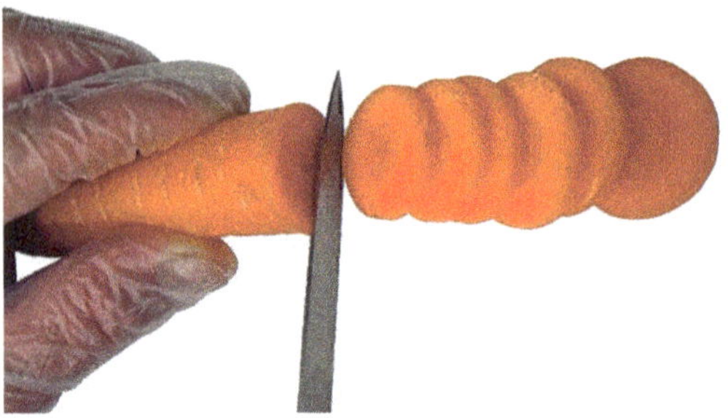

Figure 5.8 – Slice the carrots to about ¼ cm thick.

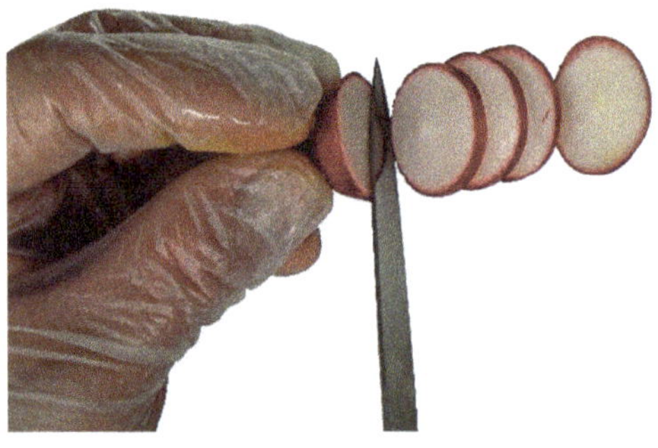

Figure 5.9 – Slice the red radish to also about ¼ cm thick.

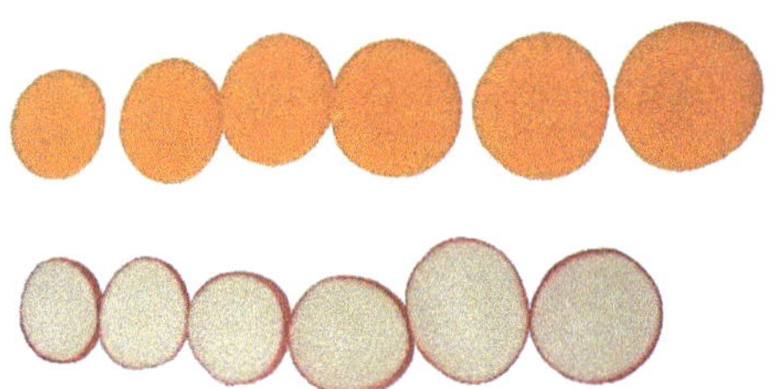

Figure 5.10 – Set aside the six slices each of carrots and radish.

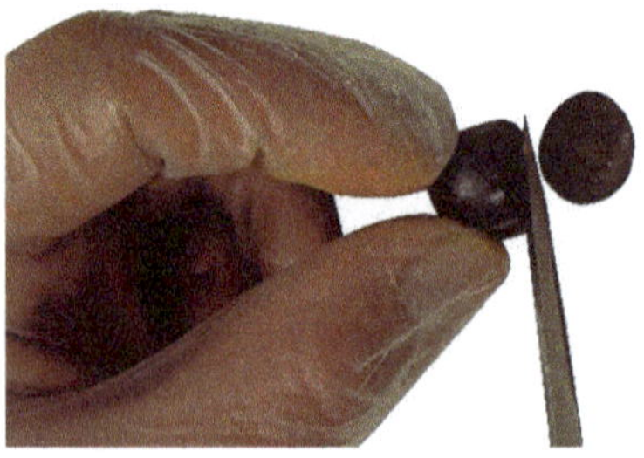

Figure 5.11 – Cut into half the 6 pcs of grapes.

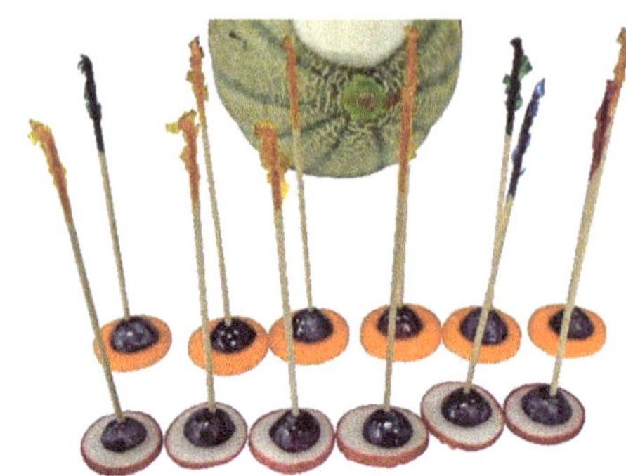

Figure 5.12 – Attach each cut grape to the slices of carrots and red radish using a cocktail toothpick.

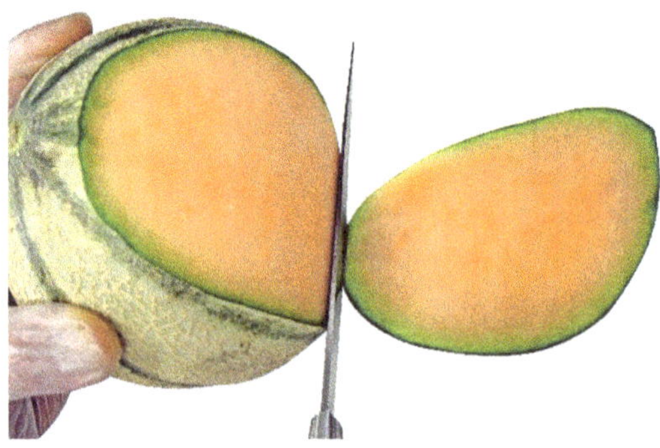

Figure 6.1 – For the wings, thickly cut the two sides of the cantaloupe.

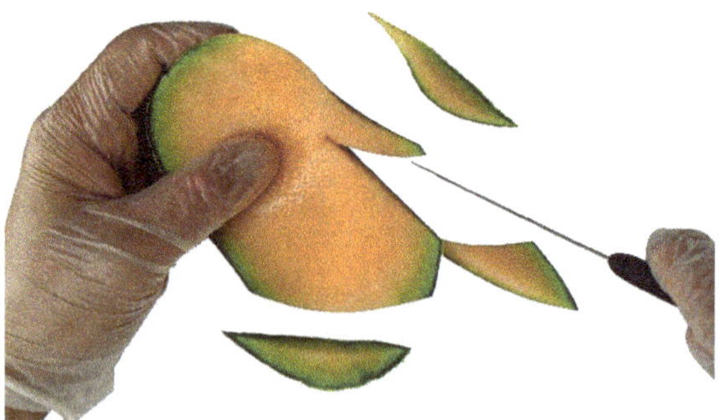

Figure 6.2 – Cut off the outer parts and shape it to look like a boxer's glove.

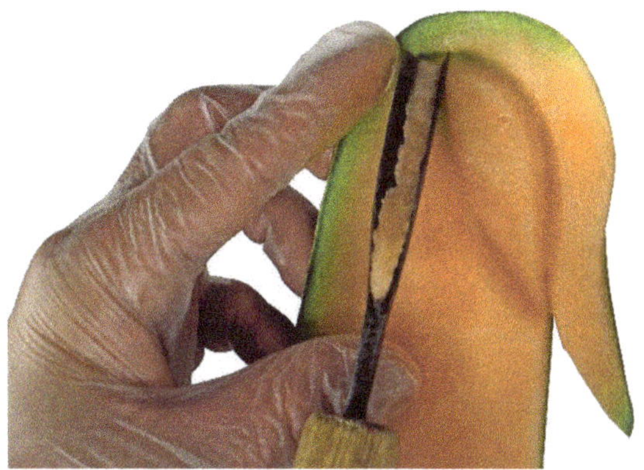

Figure 6.3 – Put the details of the wing with the use of the v-shape carving tool.

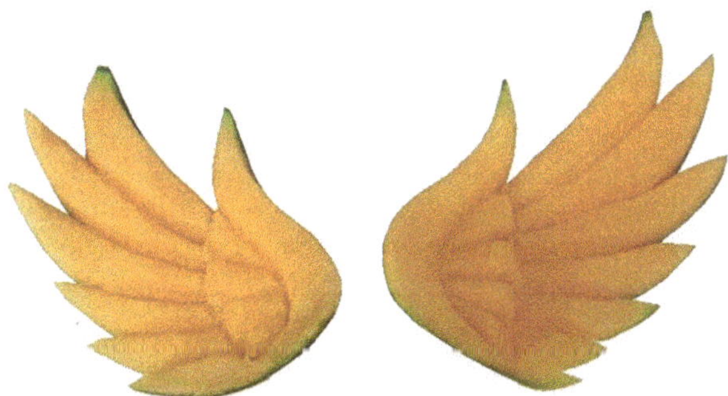

Figure 6.4 – Do the same technique to make the left and right wings as shown in the picture.

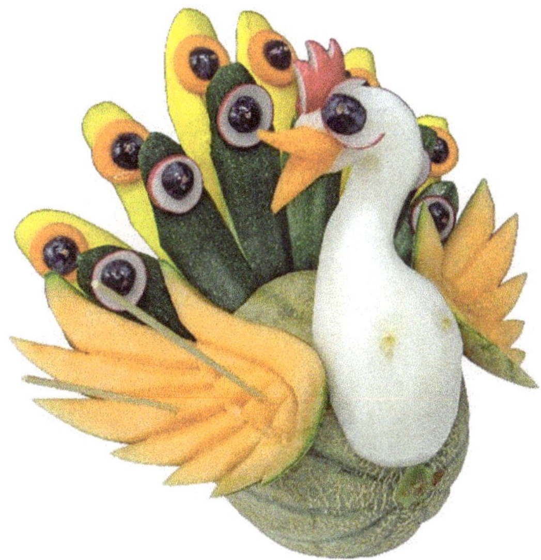

Figure 7.1 – Attach the sliced carrots with the grapes (Figure 5.12) to the yellow squash slices (first layer) and the slices of red radish with grapes to the zucchini (2nd layer) to the cantaloupe. Attach the wings using bamboo skewers as shown in the picture.

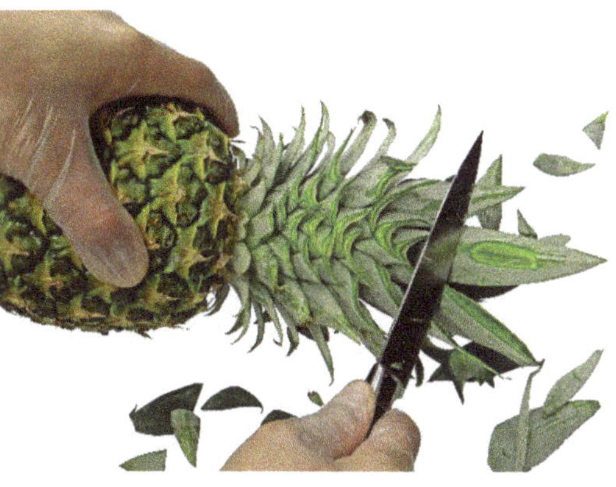

Figure 7.2 – Cut-off some parts of the pineapple leaves.

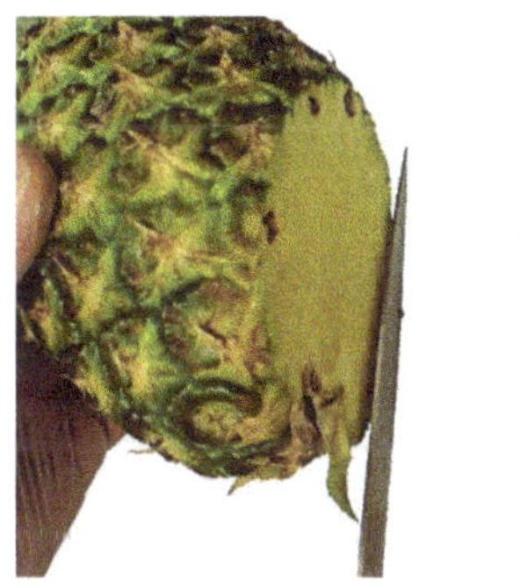

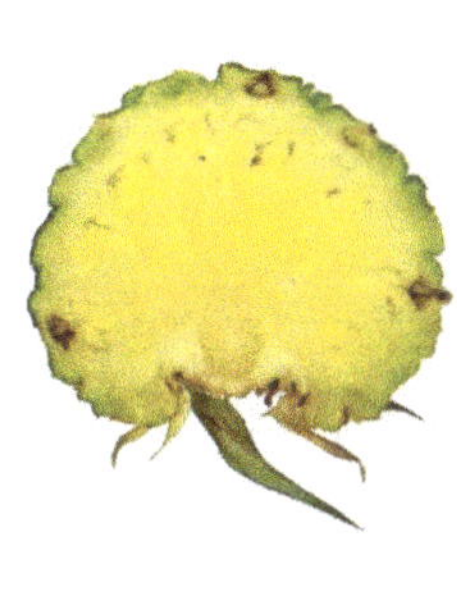

Figure 7.3 – For the base of the turkey, cut away the bottom part of the pineapple in a slanting position.

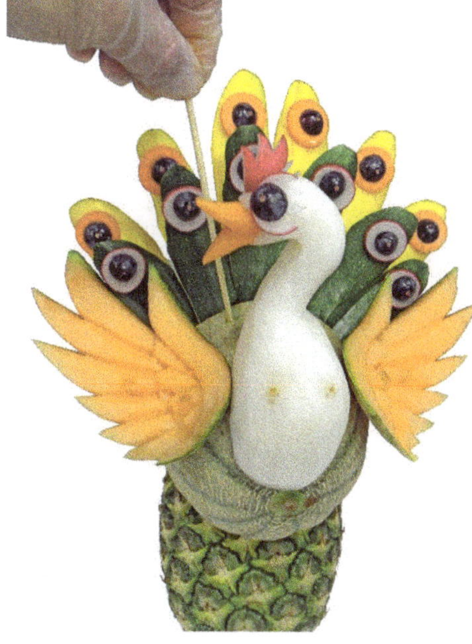

Figure 7.4 – Attach the turkey (Figure 7.1) to the pineapple using bamboo skewers.

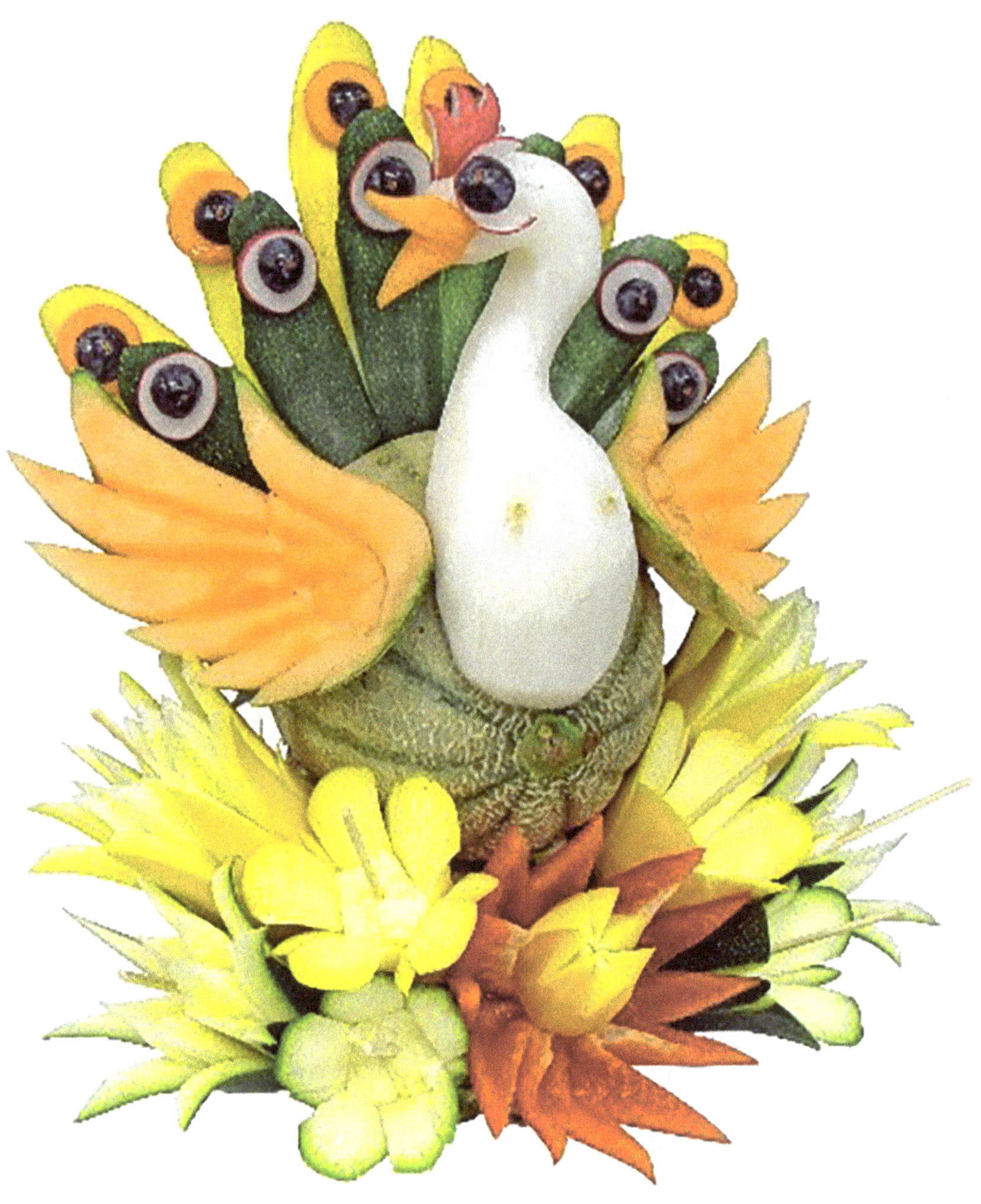

Figure 7.5 – Attach decorative flowers made out of bell pepper, yellow squash, zucchini and red radish to the base part of the pineapple.

Turkey

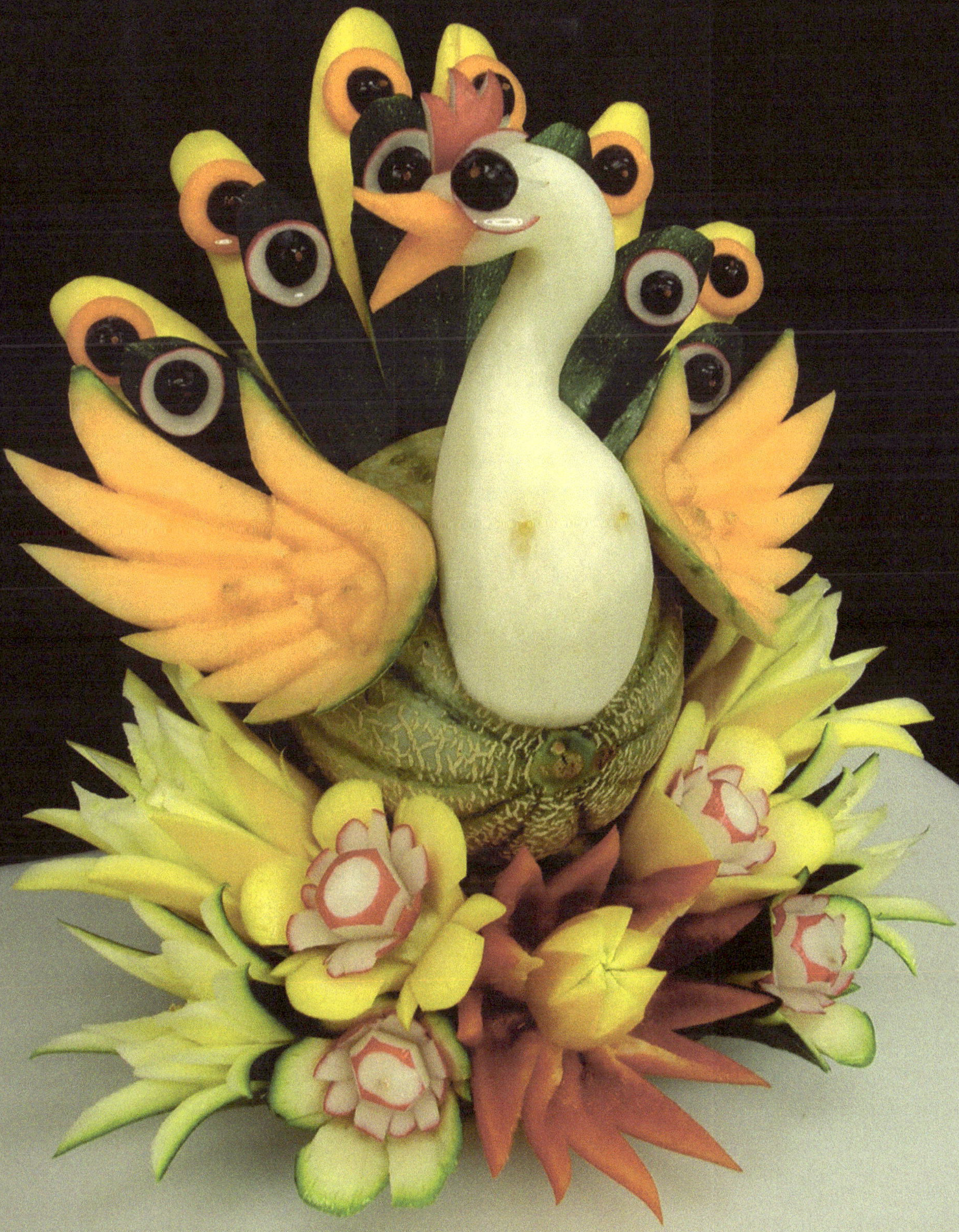

Donald Duck

This is a famous movie cartoon character which we will use for animation carving making use of fruits and vegetables. This is a perfect decoration for the cold buffet line adding attraction to your beautiful buffet and will surely amaze your guests.

Fruits, Vegetables and Materials Needed:

3 pcs grapefruits, 1 pc grape, 1 pc whole carrot, 2 pcs yellow squash, 2 pcs zucchini, 1 whole bell pepper, 1 pc pineapple, toothpicks and bamboo skewers.

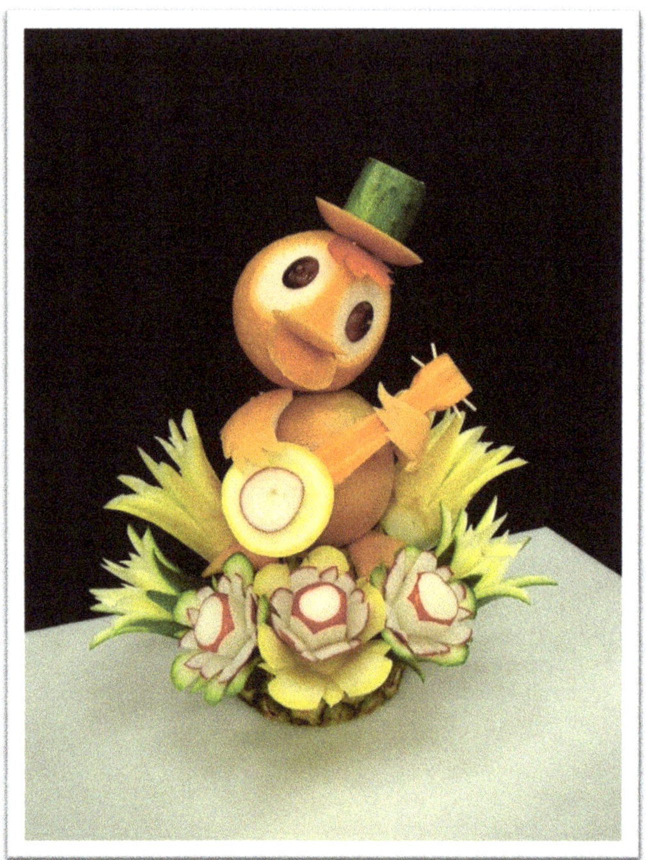

Methods and Instructions:

Figure 1.1 to 1.5 -	To make the head, beak, eyes and eyeballs
Figure 2.1 to 2.4 -	To make the body, the head and the base
Figure 3.1 to 3.6 -	To make the hat of the duck and the guitar
Figure 4.1 to 4.6 -	To make the feet, arms and hair

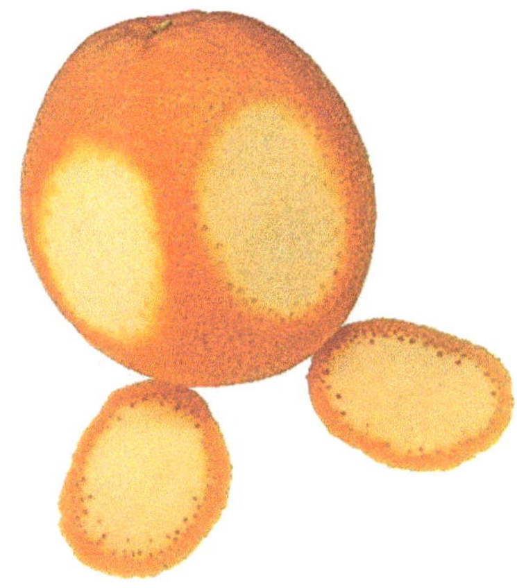

Figure 1.1 – For the eyes, cut-off two oval shapes on the grapefruit or orange skin.

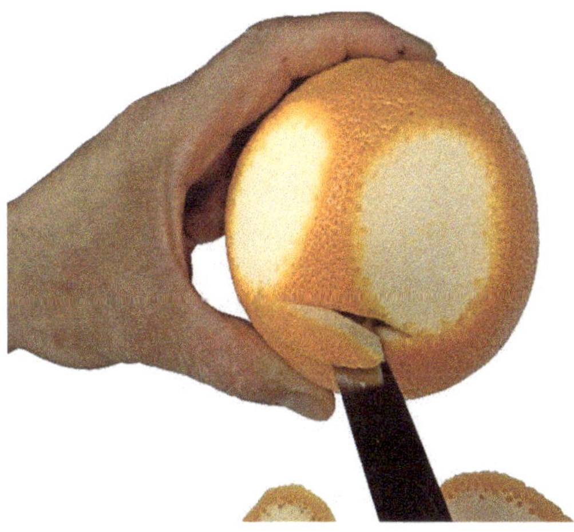

Figure 1.2 – Below both eyes, make a horizontal cut for the mouth.

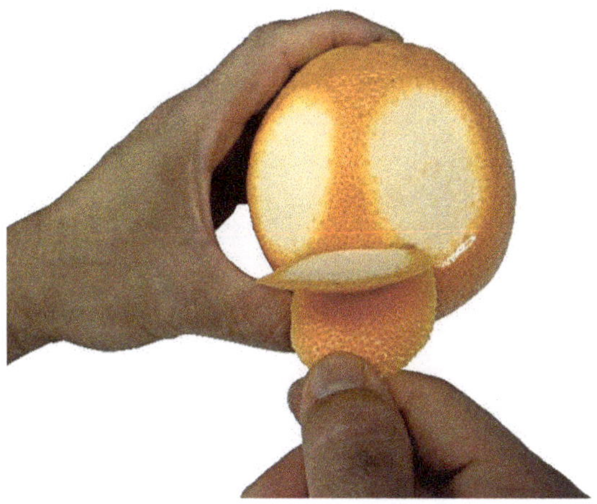

Figure 1.3 – Position the oval shaped skin of the grapefruit or orange from Figure 1.1 to Figure 1.2 as shown in the picture.

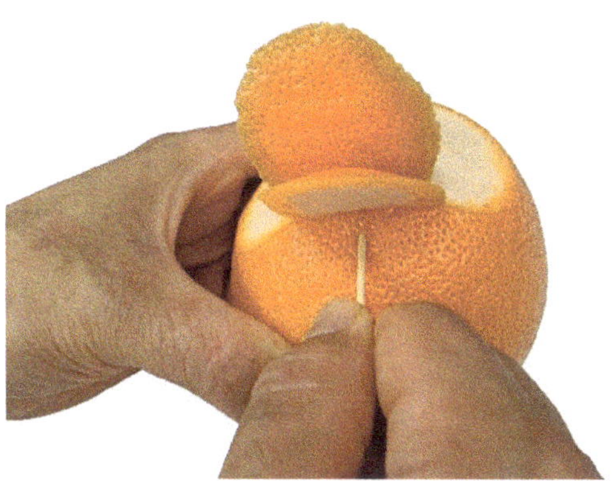

Figure 1.4 – Attach it by using a toothpick to form the beak of the duck.

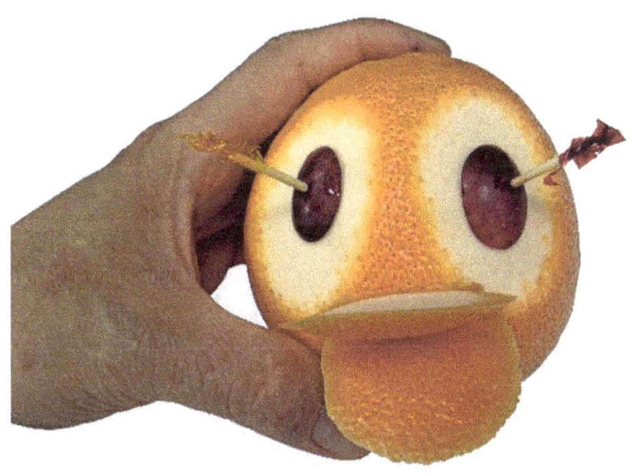

Figure 1.5 – For the eyeballs, cut lengthwise a grape in half and then attach to the center of the eyes (oval shapes) using toothpicks.

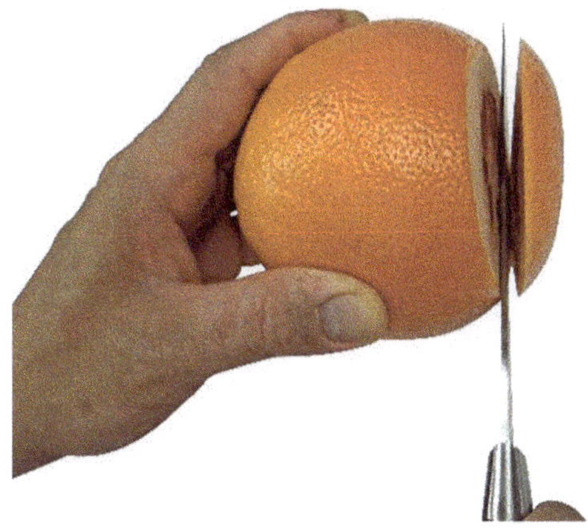

Figure 2.1 – Cut away the bottom part of another grapefruit or orange for the body of the duck. Set aside the portion that was sliced off.

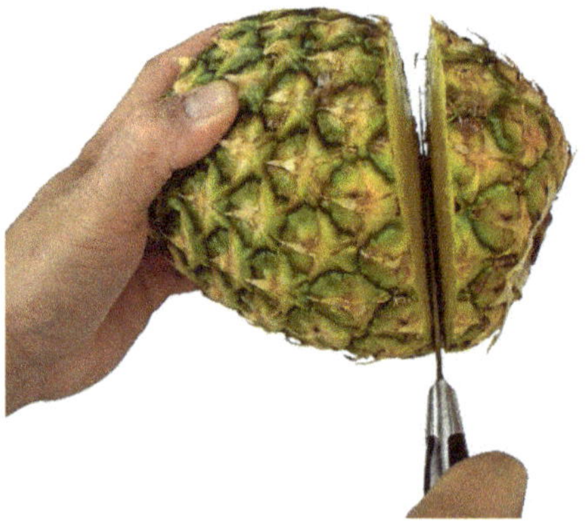

Figure 2.2 – Diagonally cut away the bottom part of the pineapple for the base of the character.

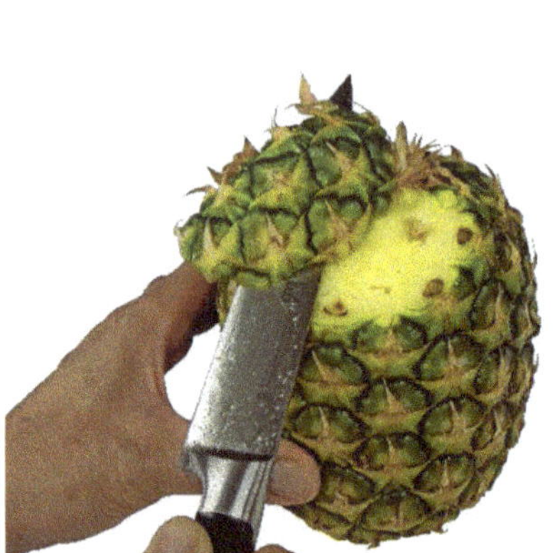

Figure 2.3 – Cut off a portion of the top of the pineapple.

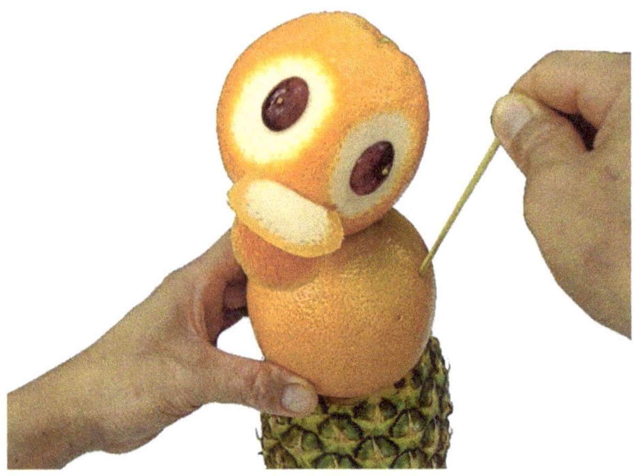

Figure 2.4 – Attach the assembled duck character on top of the pineapple using the bamboo skewers.

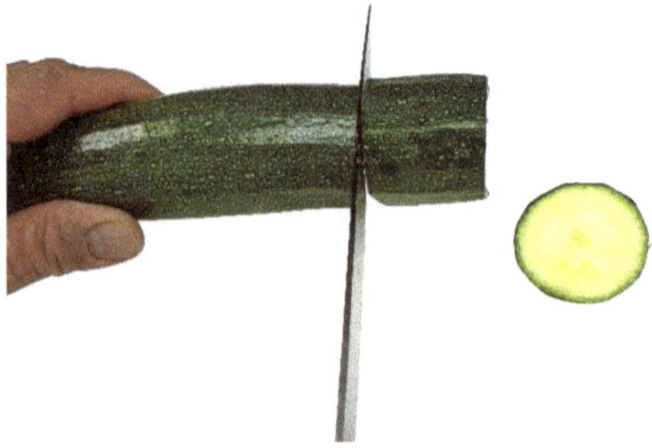

Figure 3.1 – For the hat of the duck, cut a 1 ¼ inch piece of zucchini or cucumber.

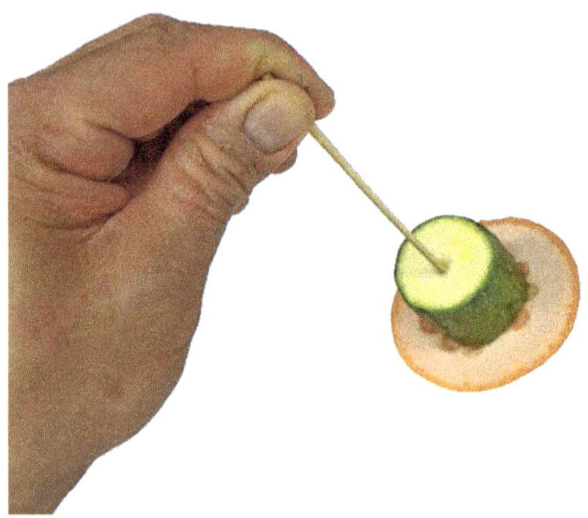

Figure 3.2 – Using the portion sliced off from Figure 2.1; attach the cut zucchini from Figure 3.1 using a bamboo skewer as shown in the picture.

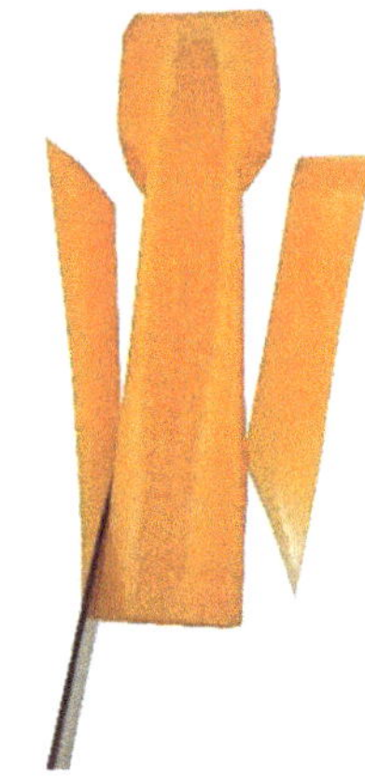

Figure 3.3 – For the handle of the guitar, shape the carrot as shown in the picture preferable with the same size.

Donald Duck

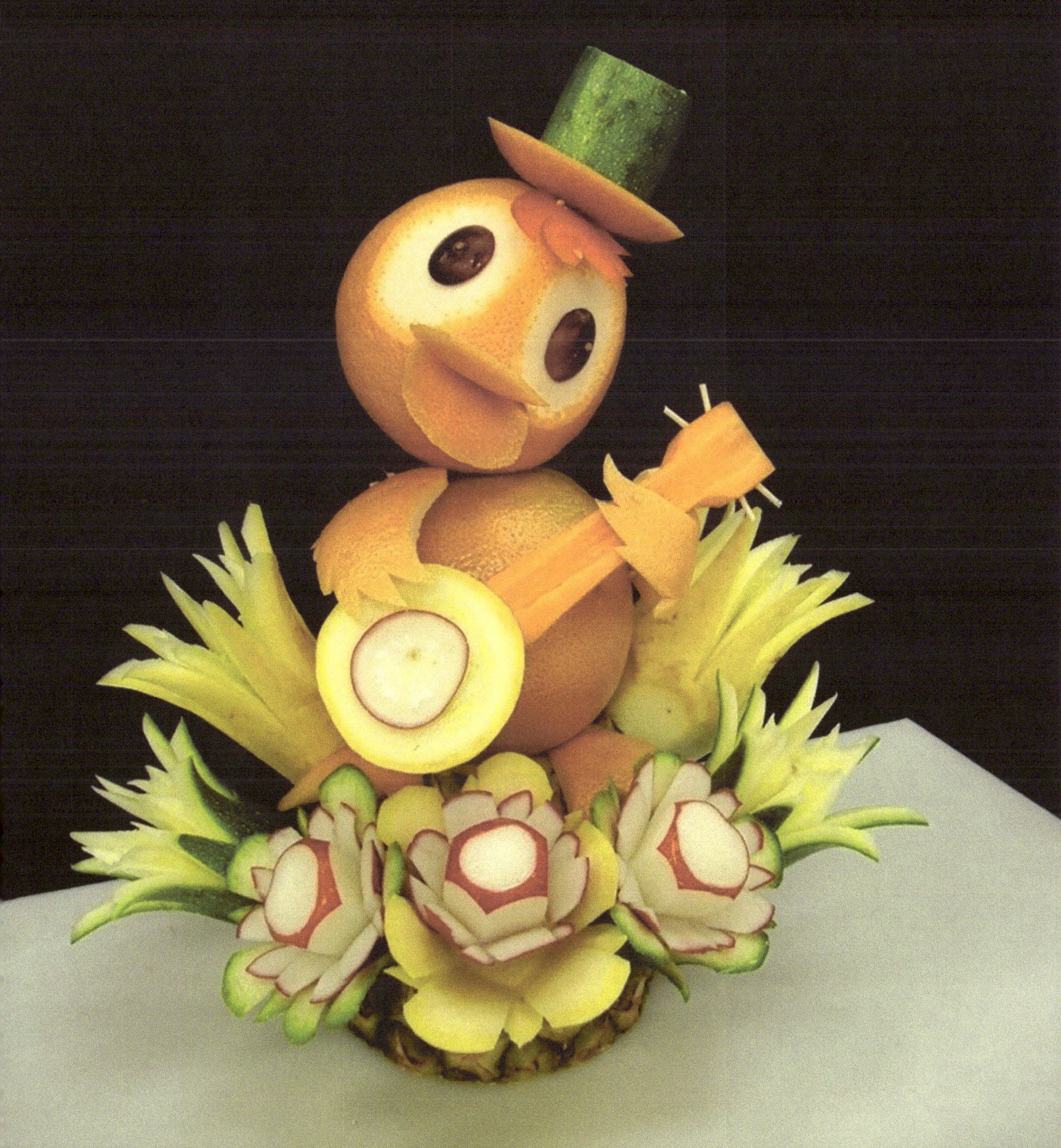

Bunny in the Barrel

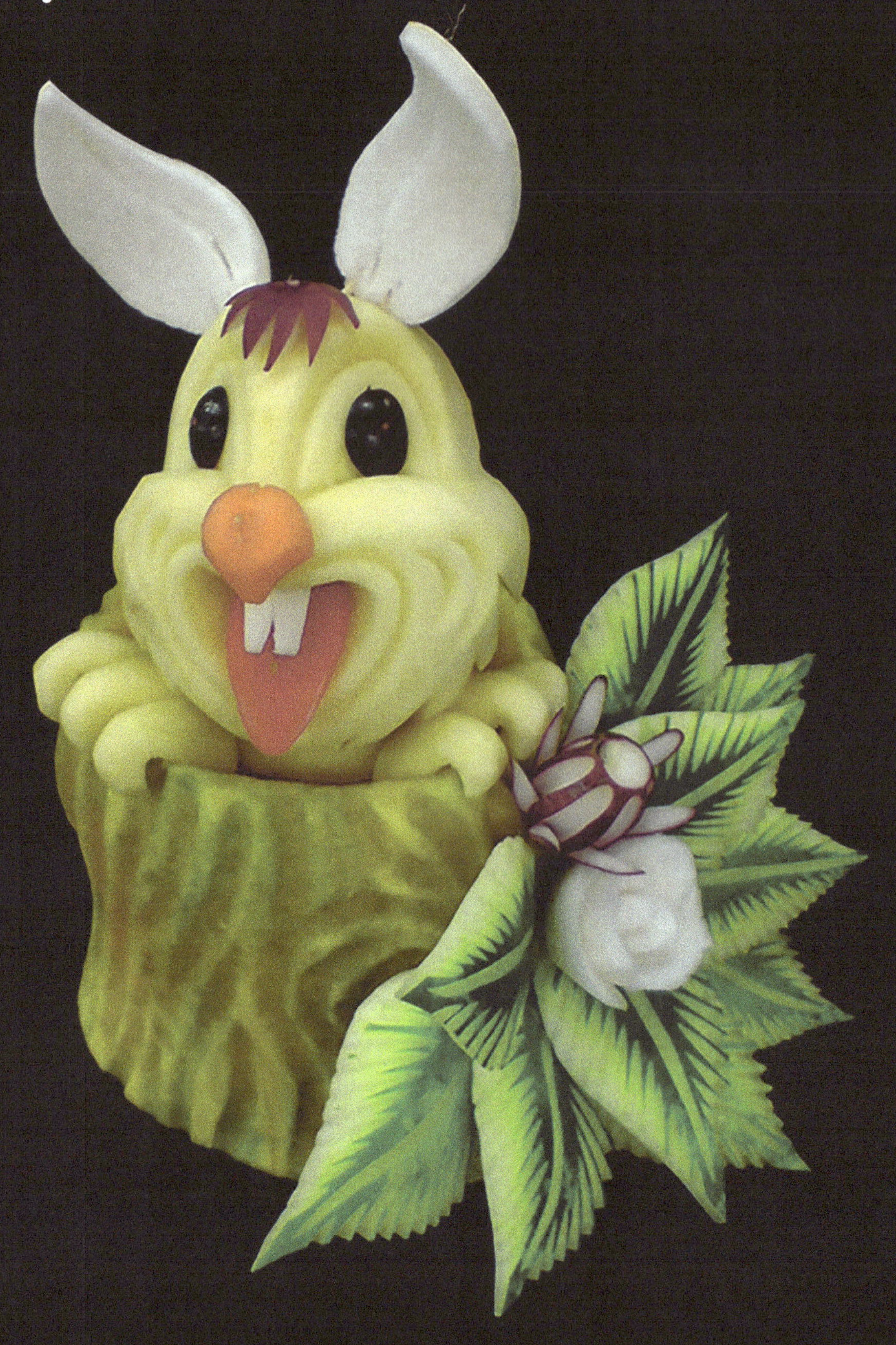

Peacock

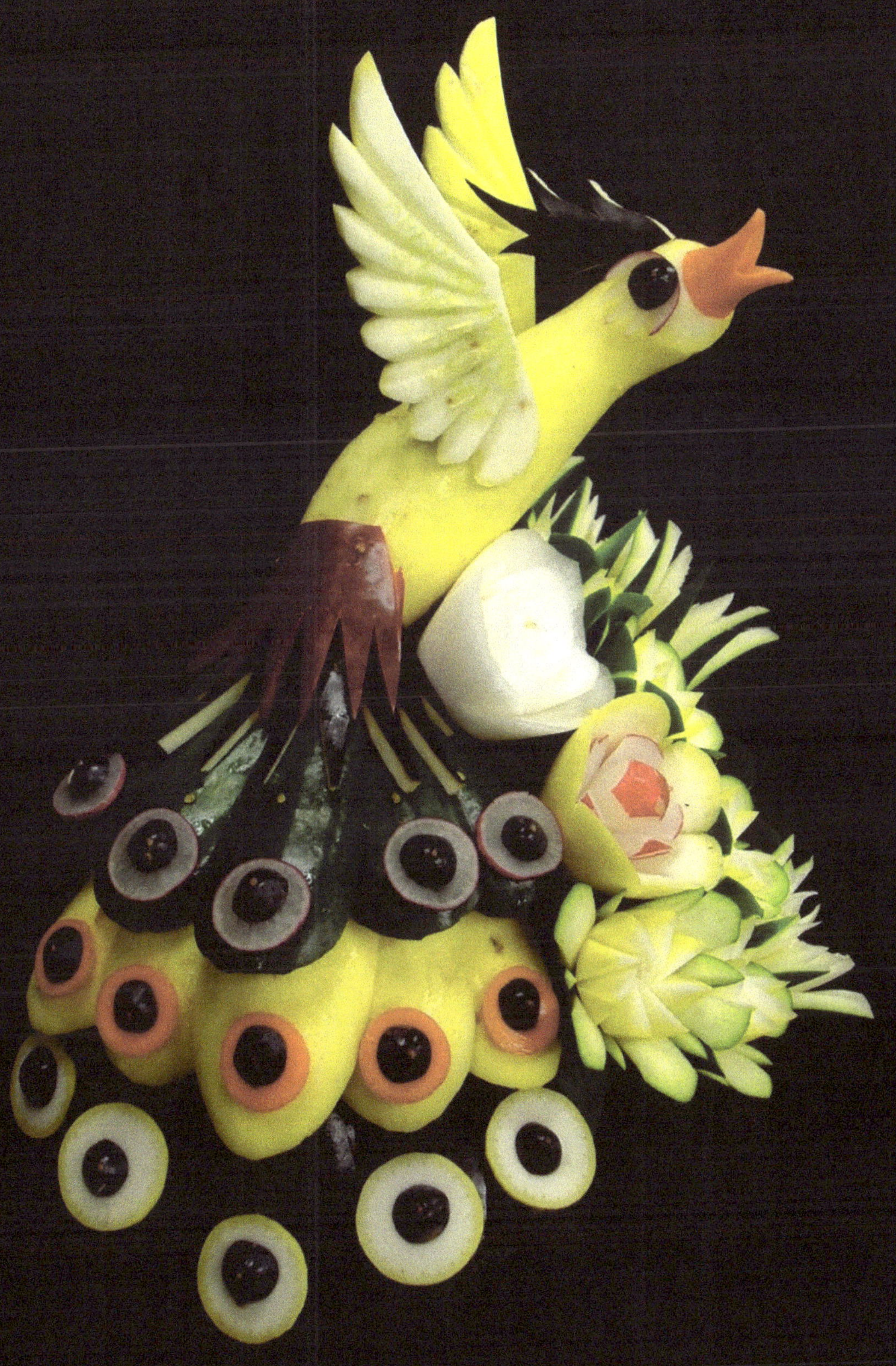

Mickey Mouse

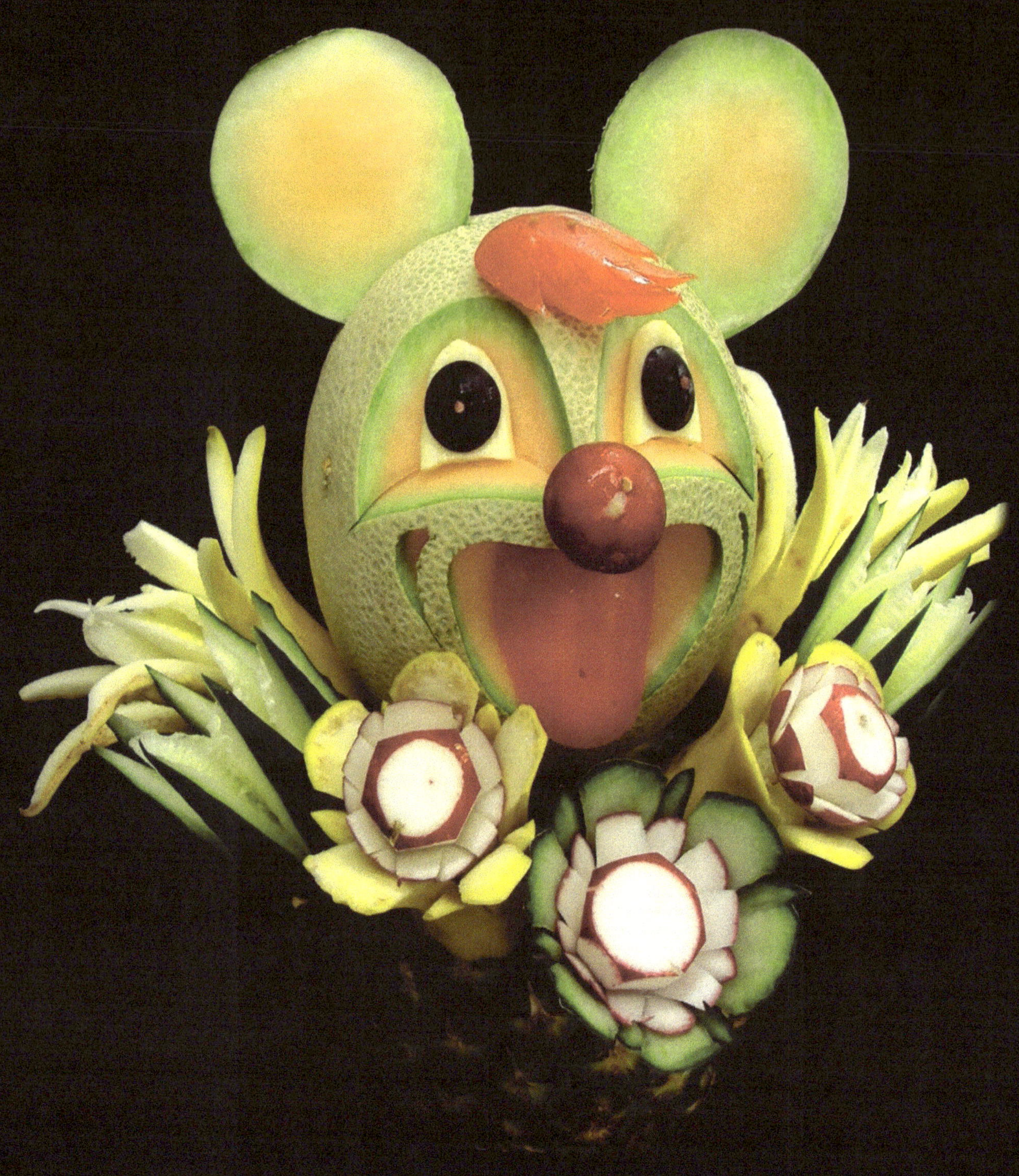

Lady Panda

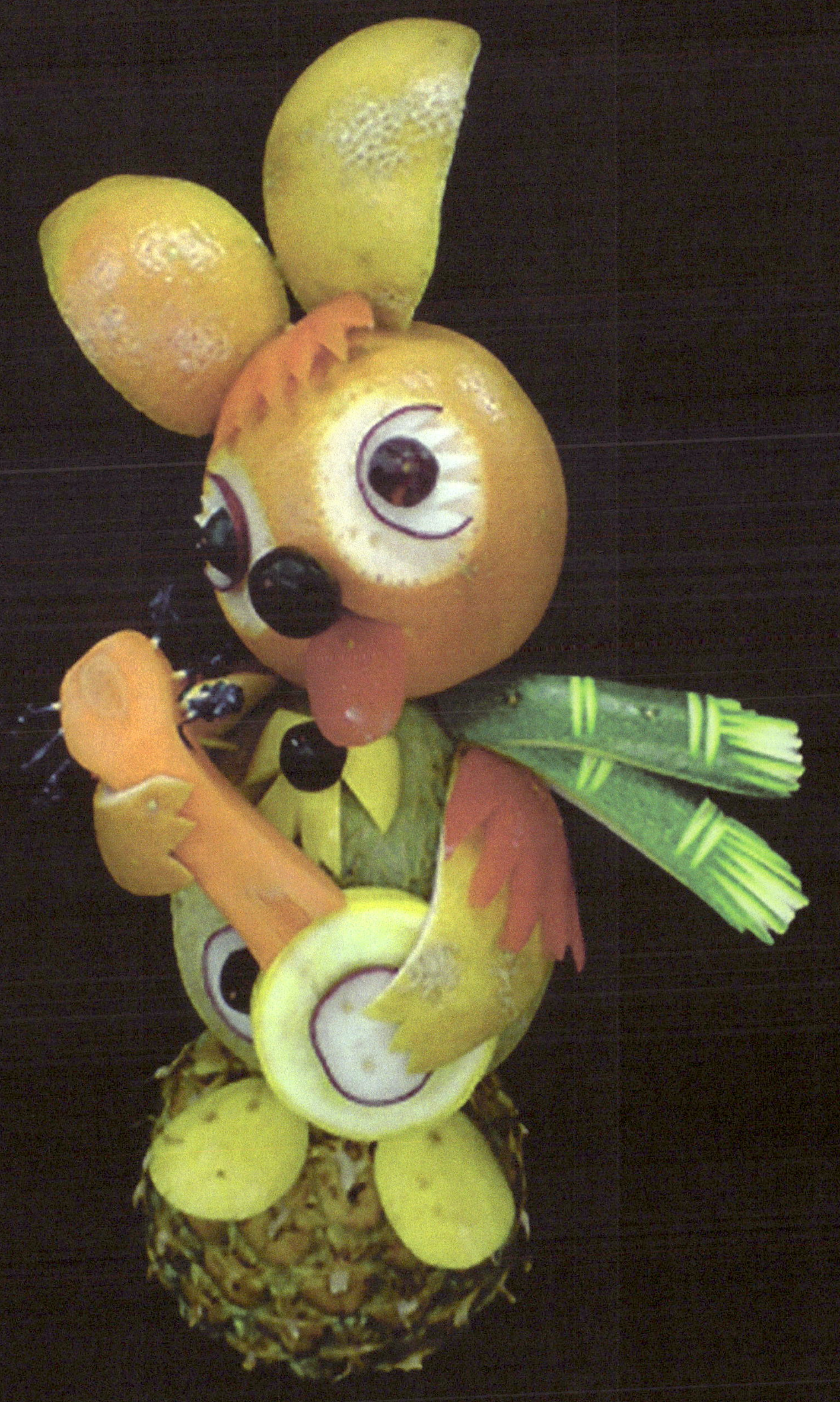

Gold Fish on Watermelon Carving

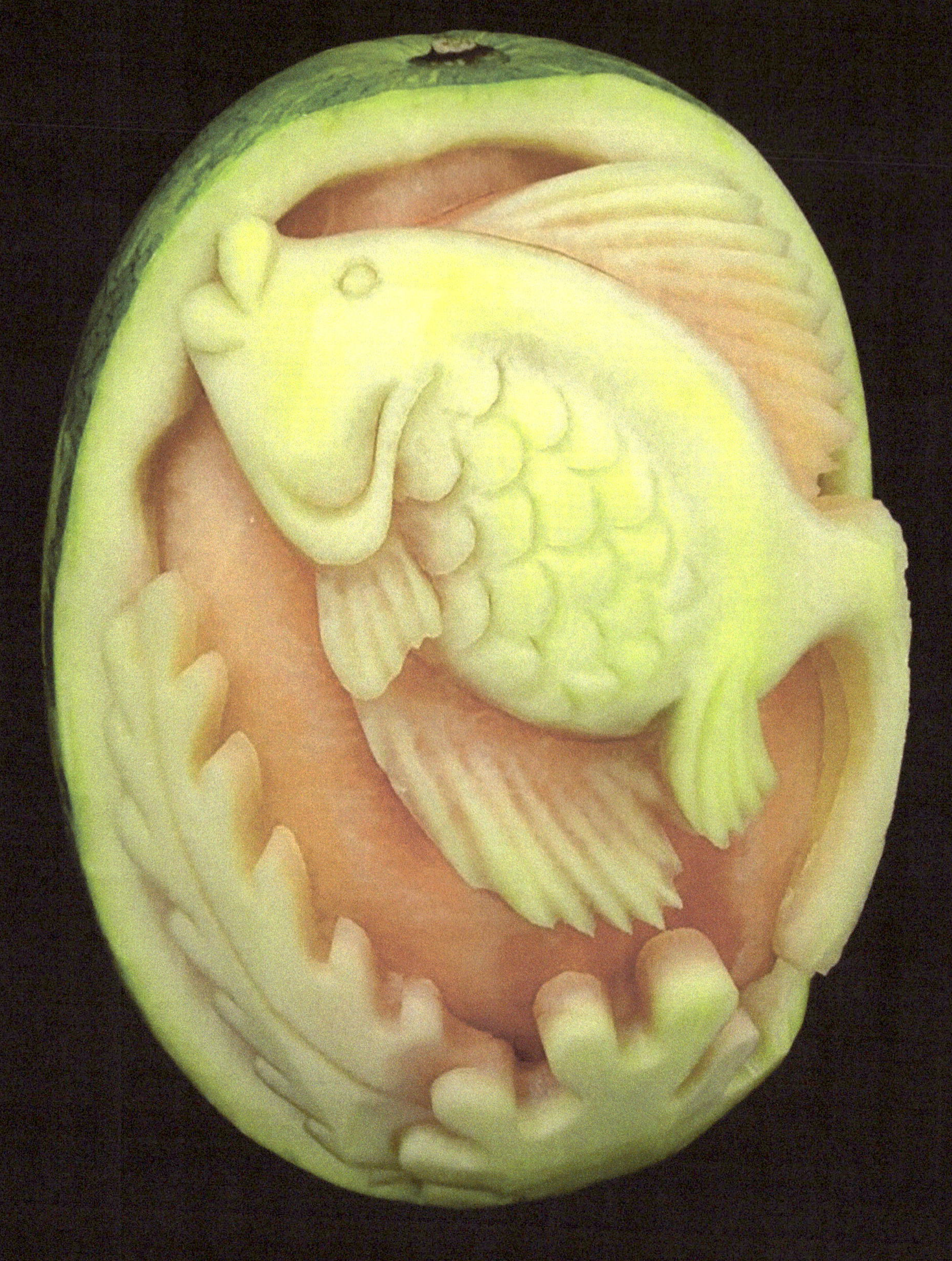

Angel Fish on Watermelon Carving

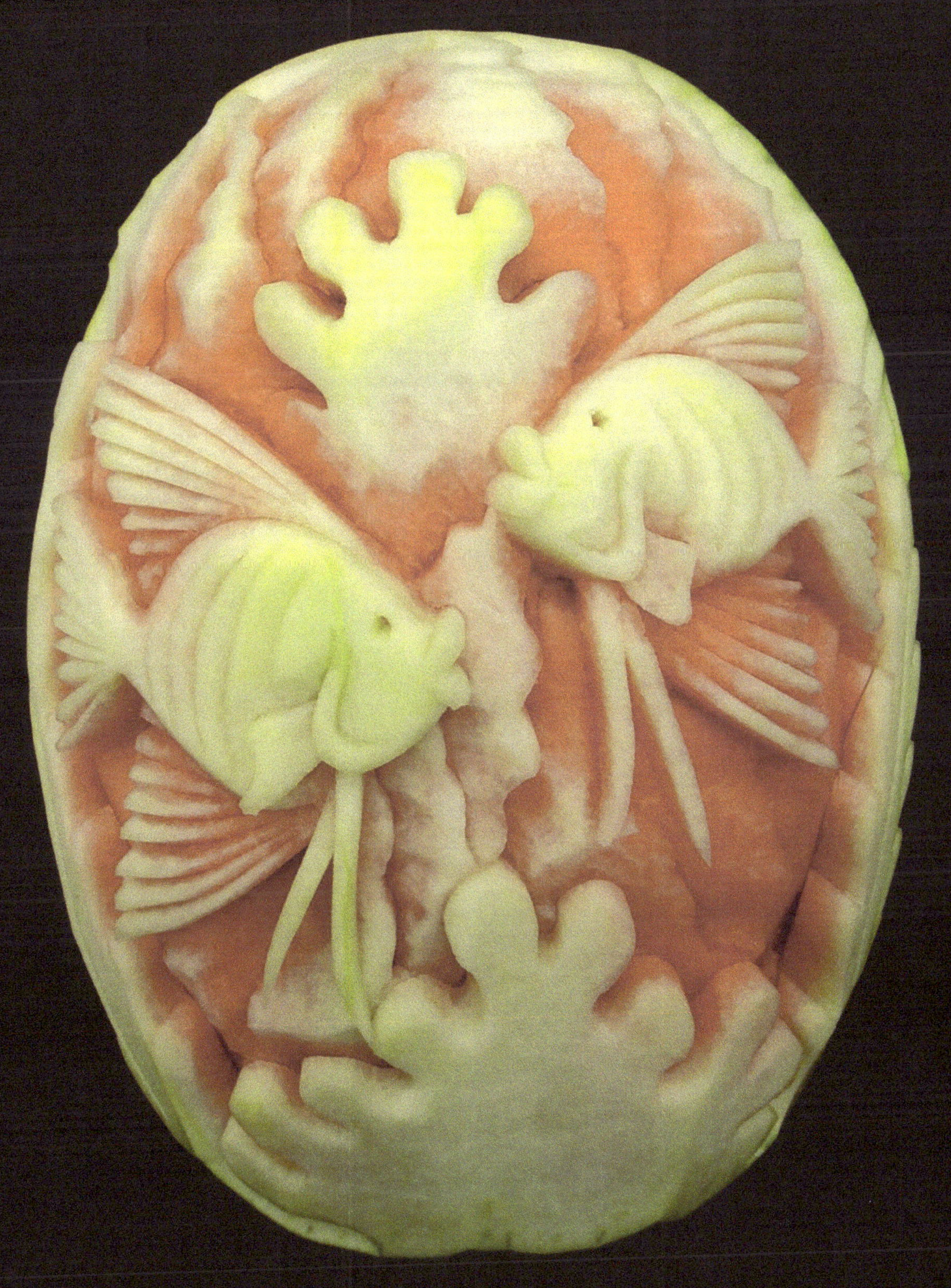

Watermelon Carving

Watermelon Carving

Basic Food Sculpture Technique

Relief Sculpture Technique

This projects a sculptured form from a flat surface. This technique requires a carving design on the surface of a watermelon. This kind of carving technique is easier than the Hallow and Round Sculpture Techniques. It is a complex form that combines many features. It is to your advantage if you have drawing skills. Remember that your pen here is your paring knife.

Hollow Sculpture Technique

This technique takes the Relief Sculpture Technique one step further. This technique is used when after carving using the Relief Structure technique; some areas need to be completely removed.

Round Sculpture Technique

This technique is more restricted in the range of its subject matter since it is more concerned with single figures and limited groups. The Relief Sculpture Technique deals with more complex subject matters.

Watermelon Carving

One of the most interesting parts of this book is learning the easy way of carving on a watermelon. With the help of your specially shaped, very sharp pointed paring knife and the touch of your carving chisel tool, you can easily acquire the knowledge and the skill on watermelon carving by just carefully following every step presented in this book.

We have been working in this field for many years now and have met many people who have shown great interest in acquiring this skill. This is the reason why we have decided to include this chapter in this book. We are simply overwhelmed whenever we receive a positive feedback.

To be able to deliver satisfaction, quality fruits and tools are necessary to be able to produce quality products. Just like some other professional culinary artists, you may experience difficulties the first time you carve a watermelon. You may first want to use honeydew or a cantaloupe as this is cheaper than the watermelon. When you follow the step-by-step procedures in this book, you will find out that engraving is not really that hard. If you have a drawing skill, think of your pointed knife as your pen.

In this chapter, we will use the Relief Sculpture Technique. Once again, remember to follow the step-by-step procedures and keep practicing until you are able to carve anything you want.

Wild Roses in Watermelon Carving

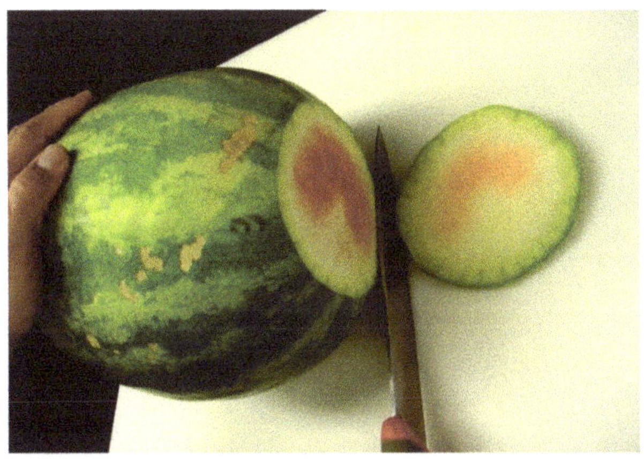

Step 1 – Cut away the bottom part of the watermelon so it will stand stable.

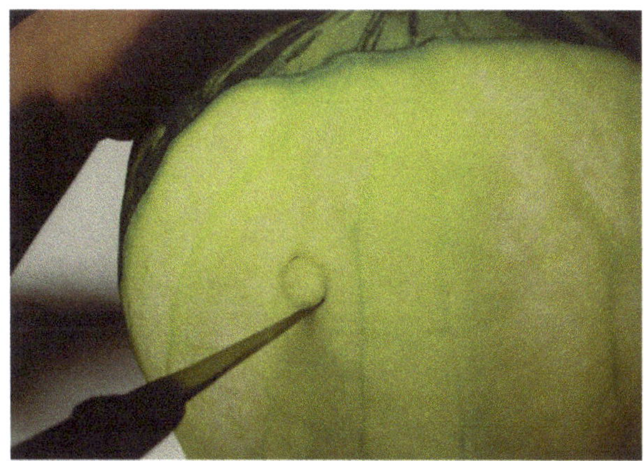

Step 4 – Draw a small circle (round) with a paring knife.

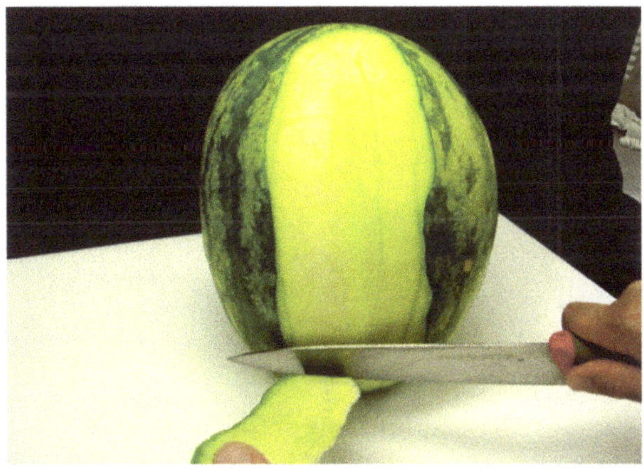

Step 2 – Remove the watermelon skin.

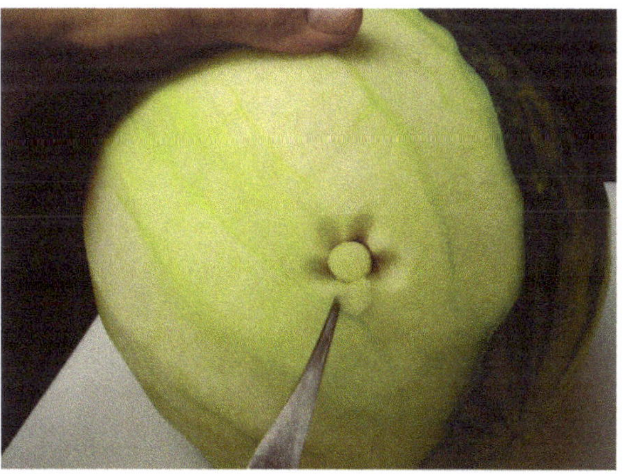

Step 5 – Carve the first layer of the petals as shown in the picture.

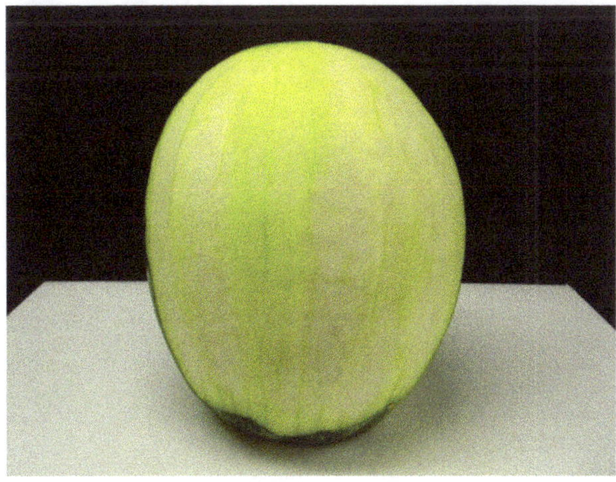

Step 3 – Remove the skin of only half of the watermelon.

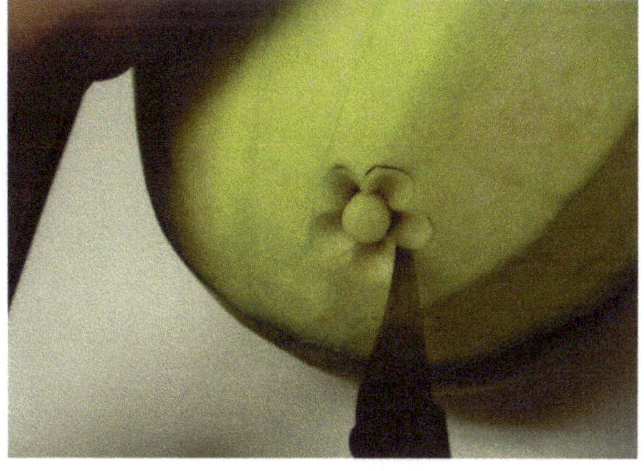

Step 6 – Draw another line behind each carved petal.

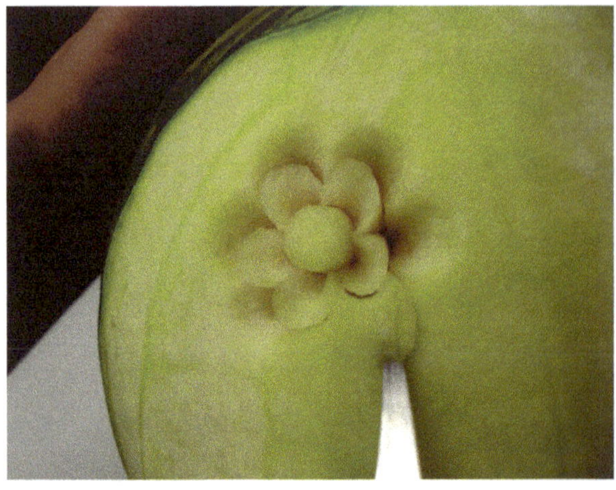

Step 7 – Carve the second layer of petals in between the first layer.

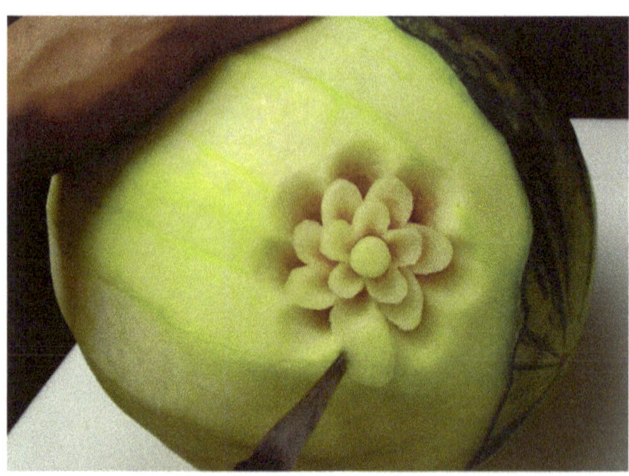

Step 10 – Continue until the third layer is completely carved.

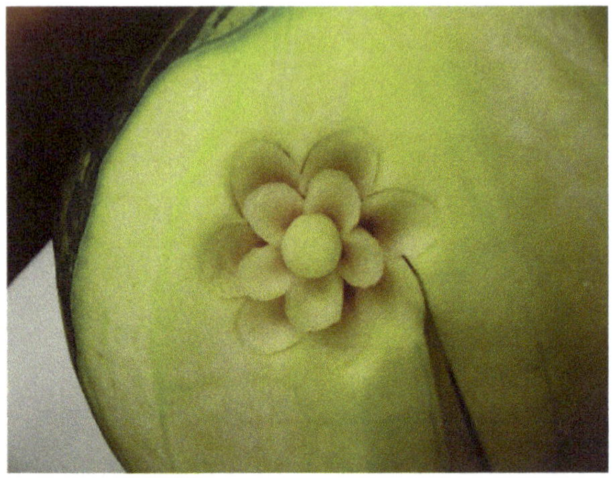

Step 8 – Behind the second layer, carve another line again

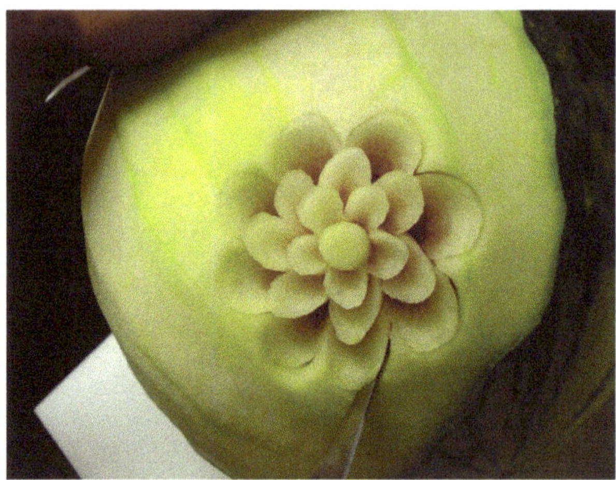

Step 11 – Continue with the same process.

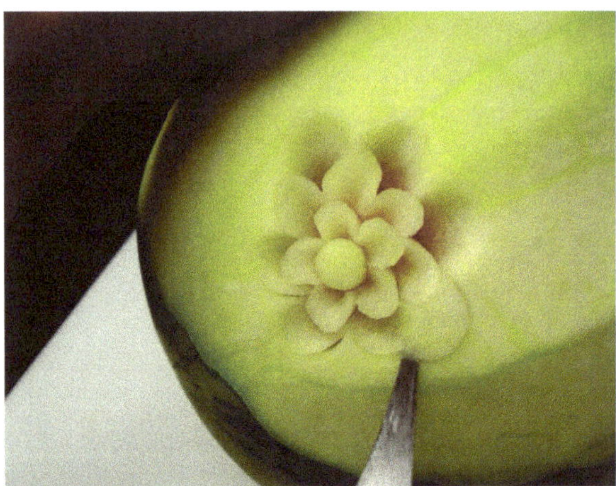

Step 9 – Carve the third layer of petals

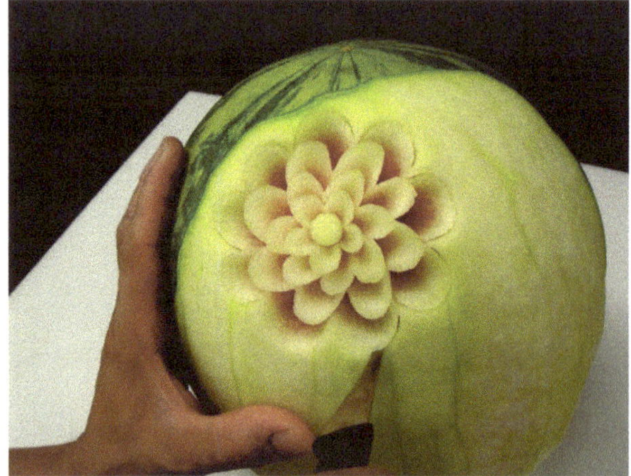

Step 12 – After the fourth layer of petals, leave the mark of your knife behind it as shown in the picture.

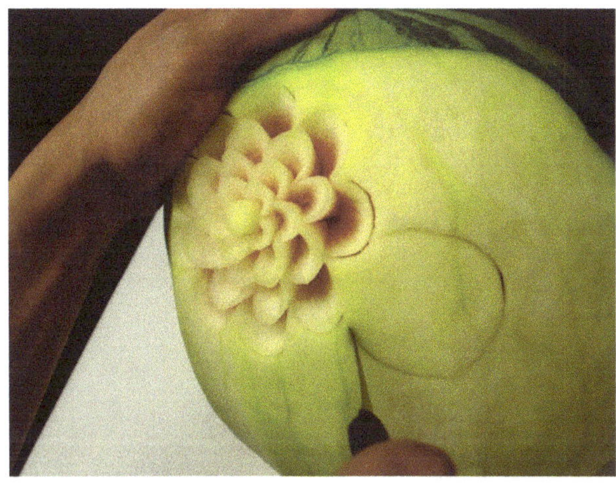

Step 13-Draw a circle besides the first flower that you make.

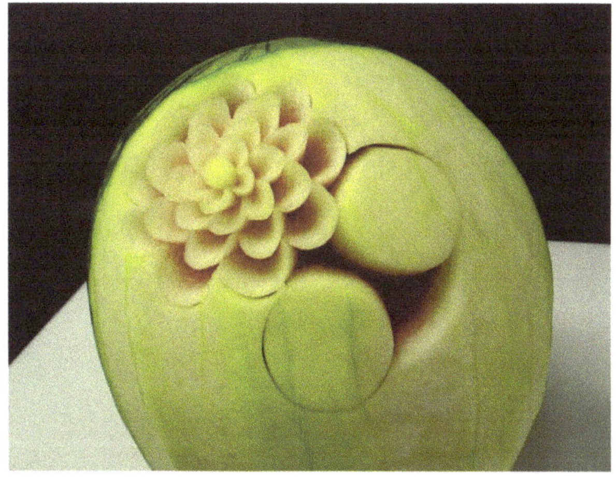

Step 16 – Check out how much deeper you need to carve.

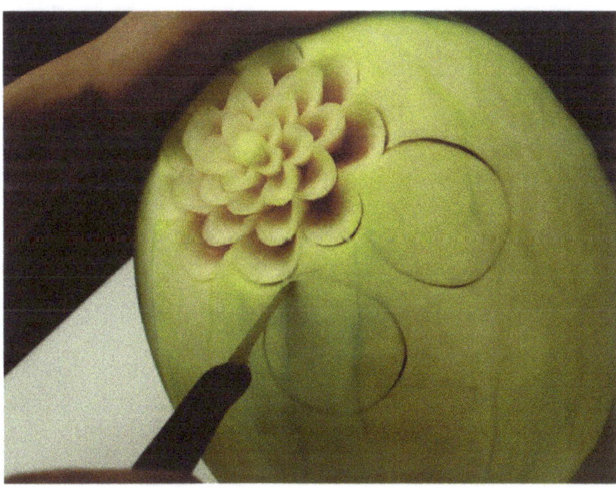

Step 14 – Draw a second circle below the first circle.

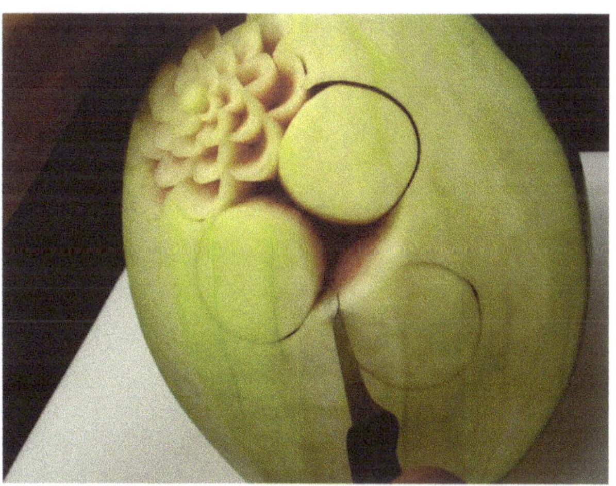

Step 17 – Draw a third circle between the lower portions of the two circles.

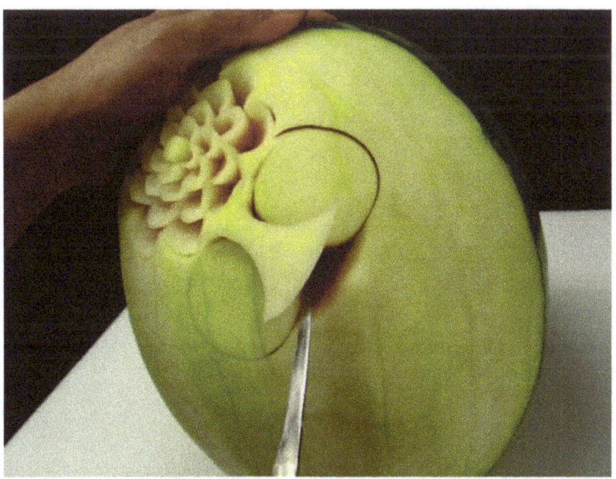

Step 15 – Remove the watermelon flesh between the two circles.

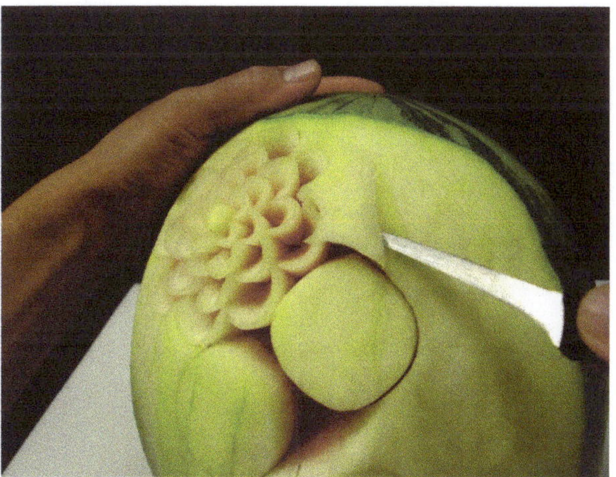

Step 18 – Start to remove the watermelon flesh on that portion on the sides of the circle as shown in the picture.

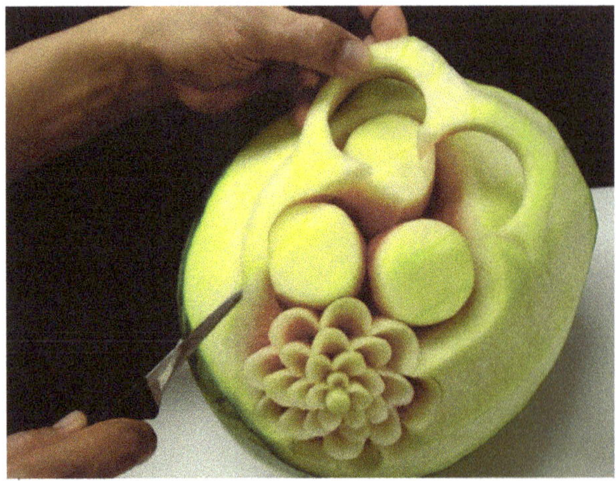

Step 19 – Continue to remove the sides around the three (3) circles.

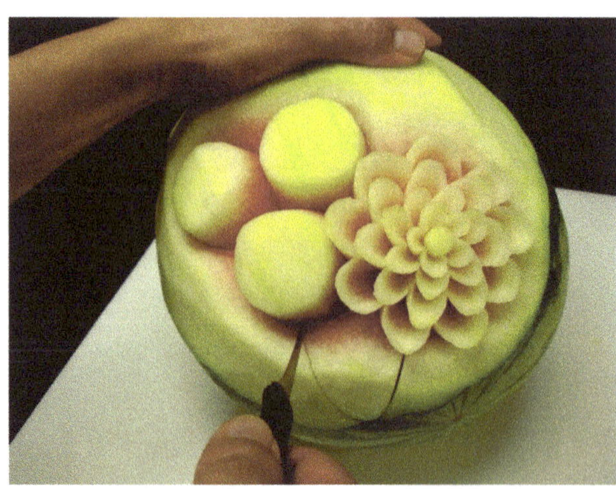

Step 22 – Make a U-shape cut as shown in the picture.

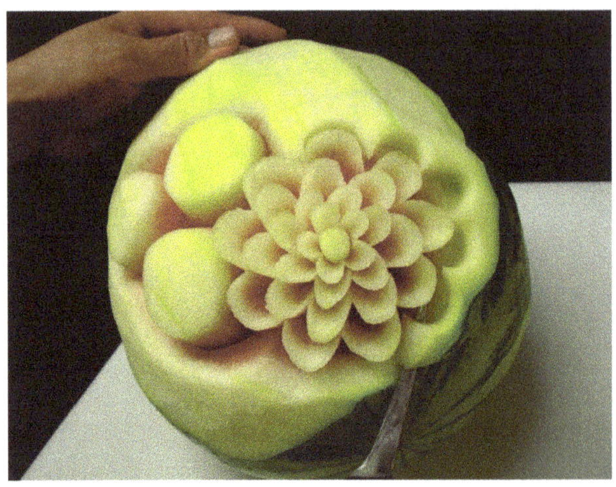

Step 20 – Remove also the watermelon flesh on the sides of the first flower.

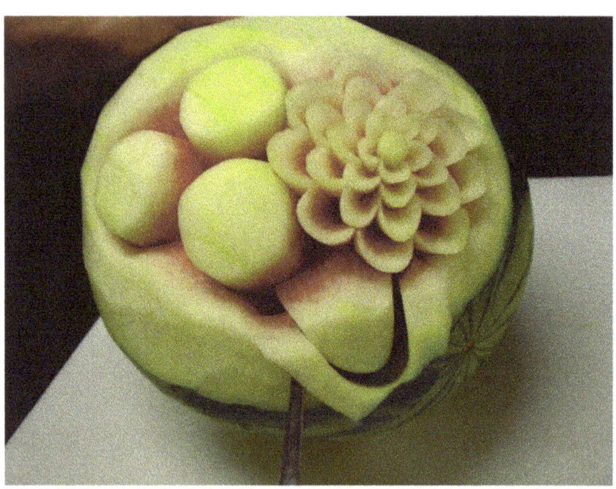

Step 23 – Remove the watermelon flesh around the outside portion of the U-shape.

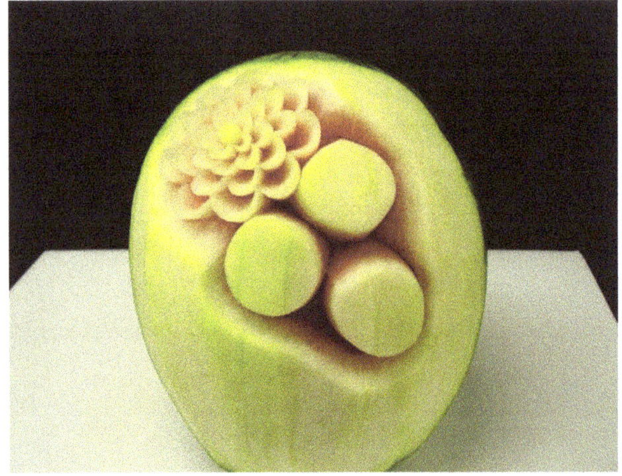

Step 21 – Continue until you have completely removed watermelon flesh on the inside and outside portions of the circle.

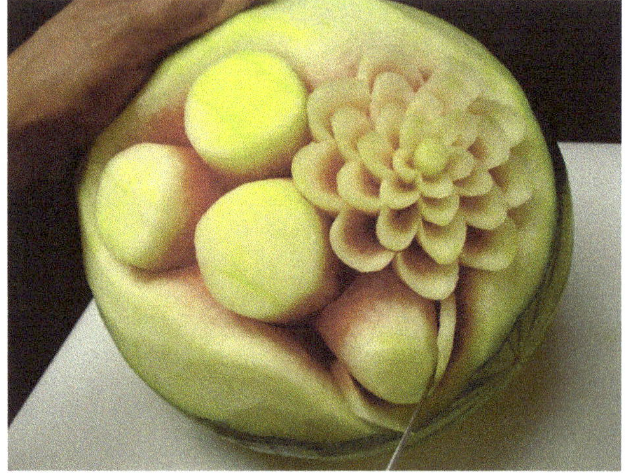

Step 24 – Remove the sharp edge of the U-shape.

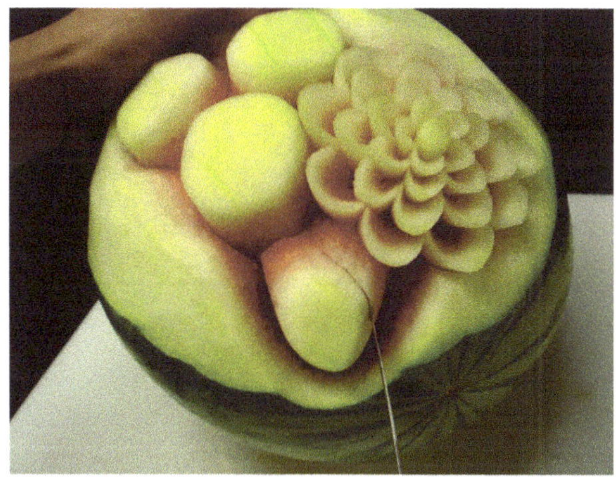

Step 25 – Draw a line on the right side of the U-shape.

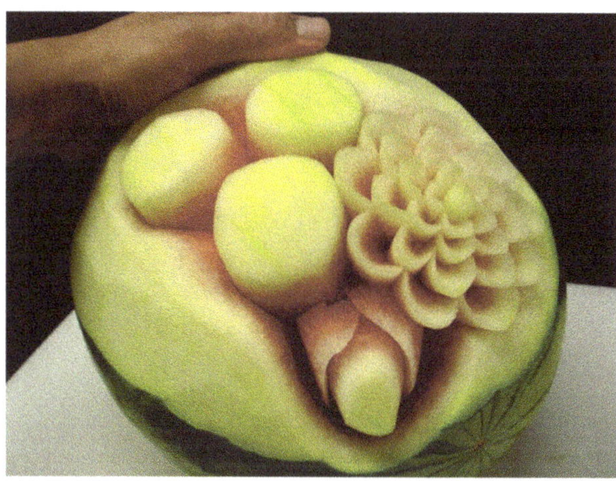

Step 28 – Remove the watermelon flesh on the inside part of the left side line as shown in the picture.

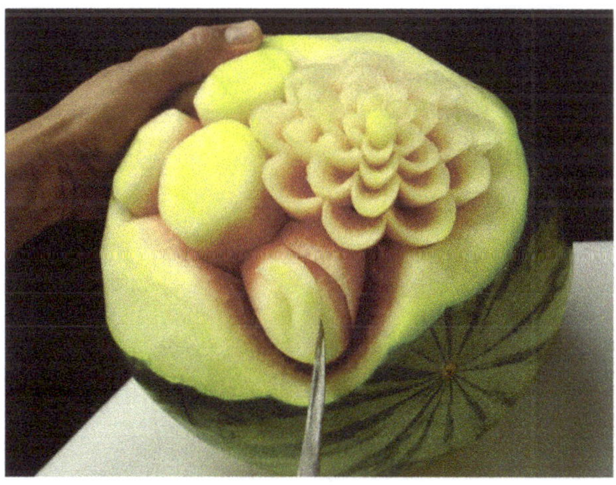

Step 26 – Remove the watermelon flesh on the inside part of the line you made.

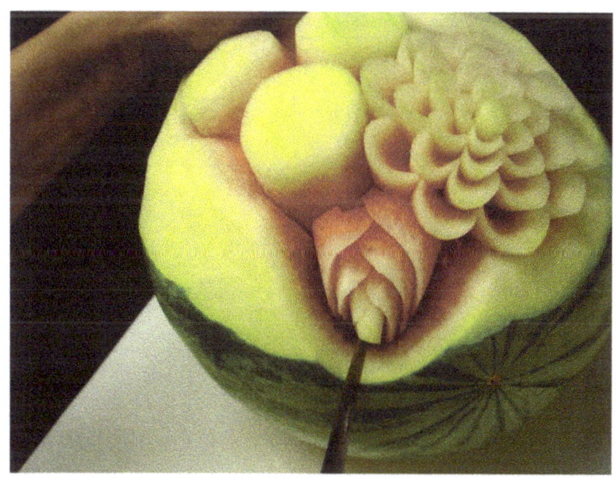

Step 29 – Continue to do the same process below the first two (2) lines that you have done.

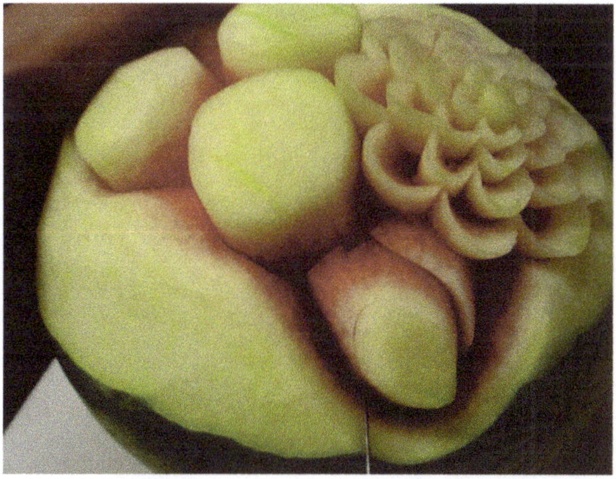

Step 27 – Draw another line on the left side of the U-shape.

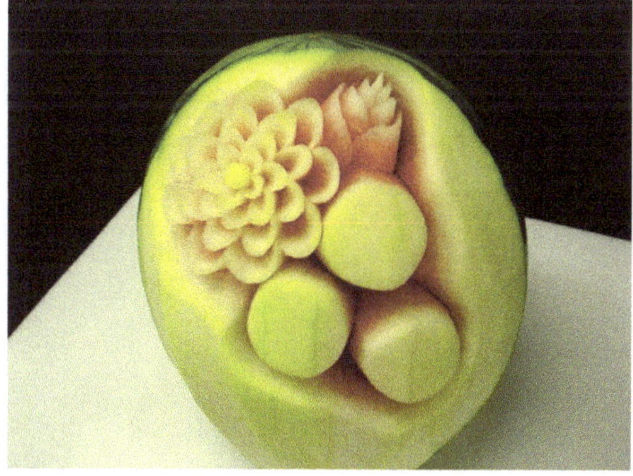

Step 30 – Continue the procedure until you have formed a young rose flower.

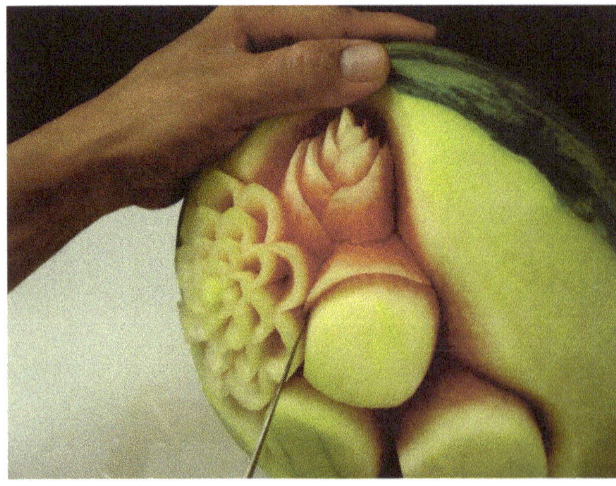

Step 31 – Draw a C-shaped line on the side of the circle as shown in the picture. Open it by removing the watermelon flesh inside.

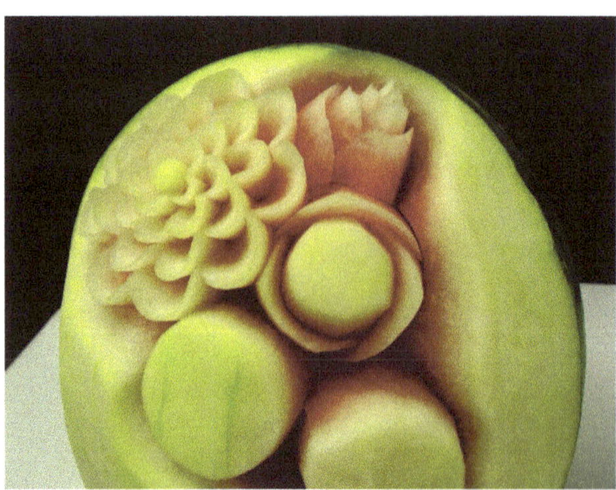

Step 34 – Do the same procedure and make the third C-shaped line on the side of the circle.

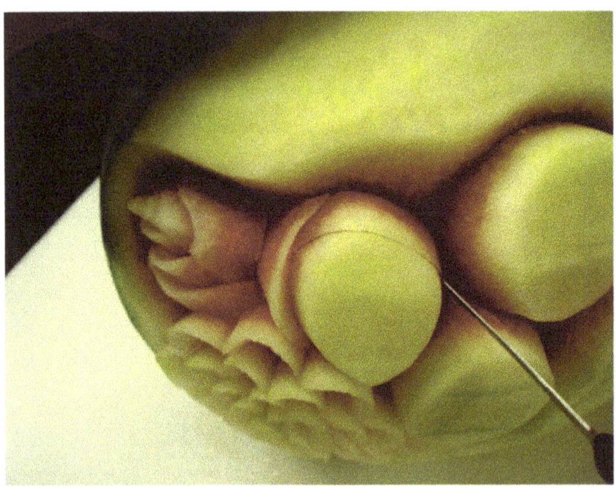

Step 32 – Starting from the middle portion of the first cut, draw and cut another C-shaped line.

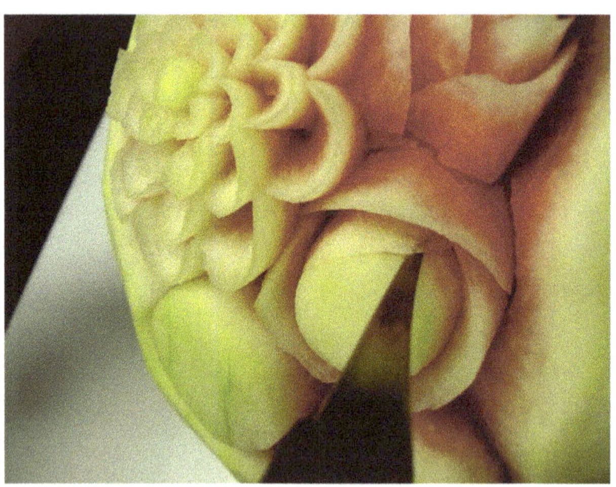

Step 35 – Between the two (2) outside petals, draw another layer on it as shown in the picture.

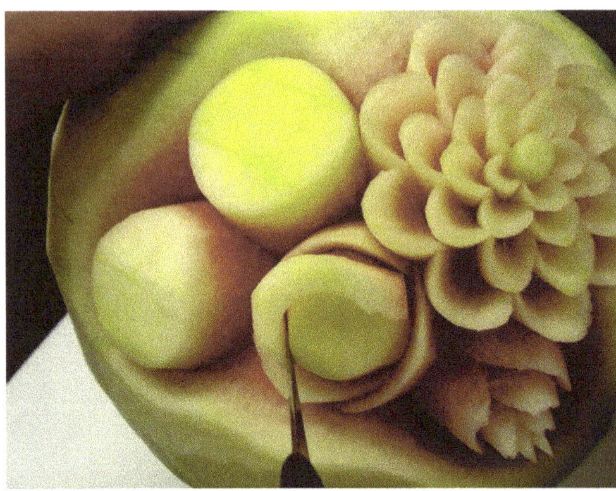

Step 33 – Remove the watermelon flesh inside to open it.

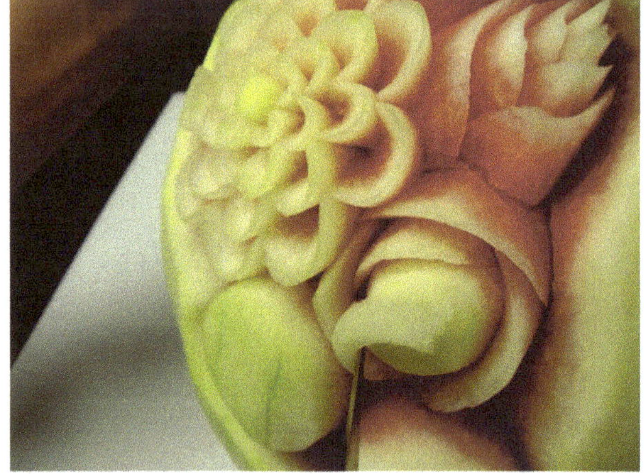

Step 36 – Remove the watermelon flesh from the inside part then form the next two (2) petals to complete the second layer.

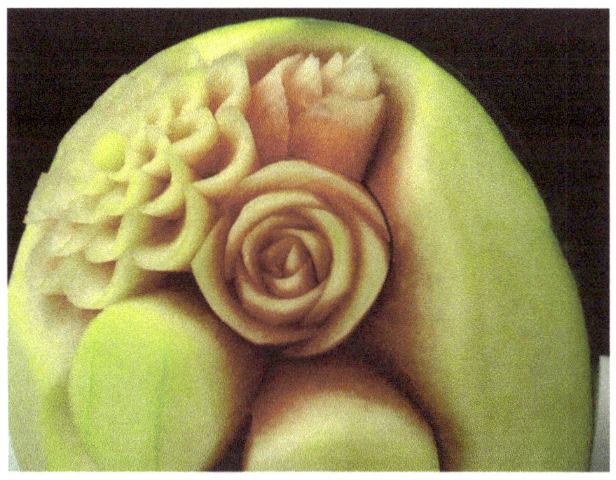

Step 37 – As you can see, the same process was used from the outside to the inside part of the circle.

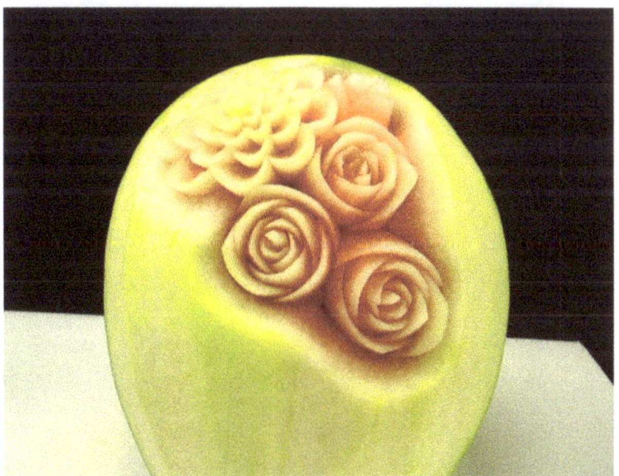

Step 38- Continue until you have three red roses.

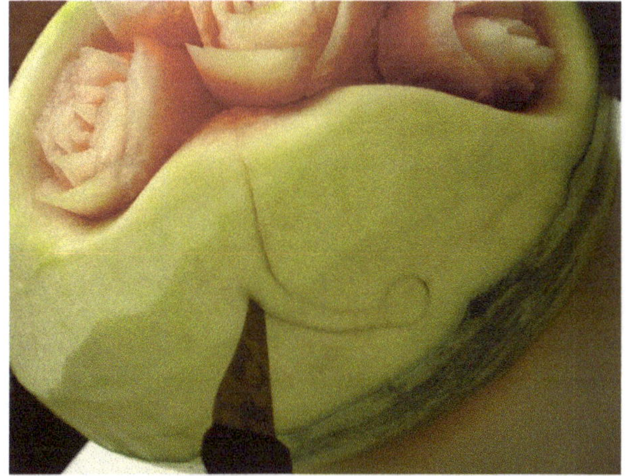

Step 39 – Draw a flower cone starting between the two roses.

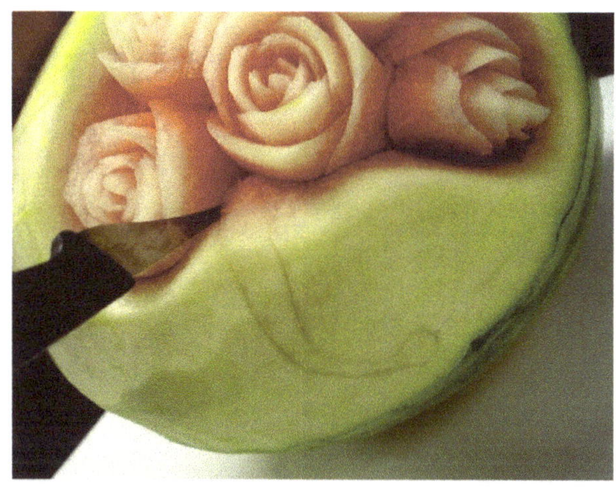

Step 40 – Calculate how deep you need to go when you put in the paring knife.

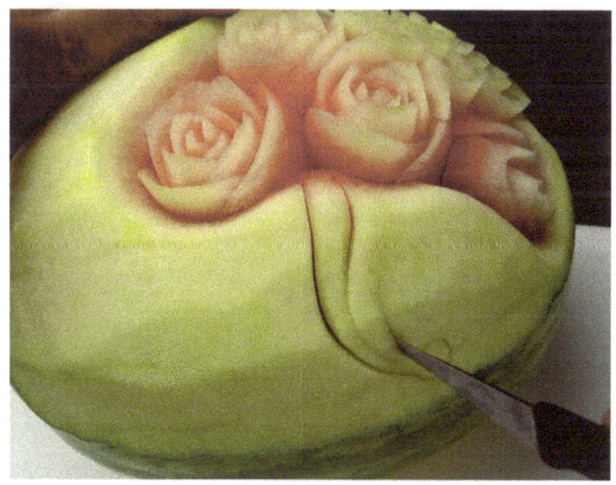

Step 41 – Remove the flesh on the side of the cone.

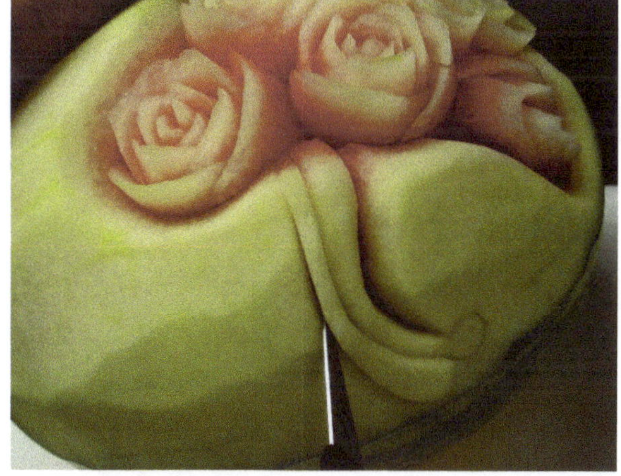

Step 42 – Do the same on the other side to make the cone clear.

How to engrave the Lily Flower
on the sides of the Roses

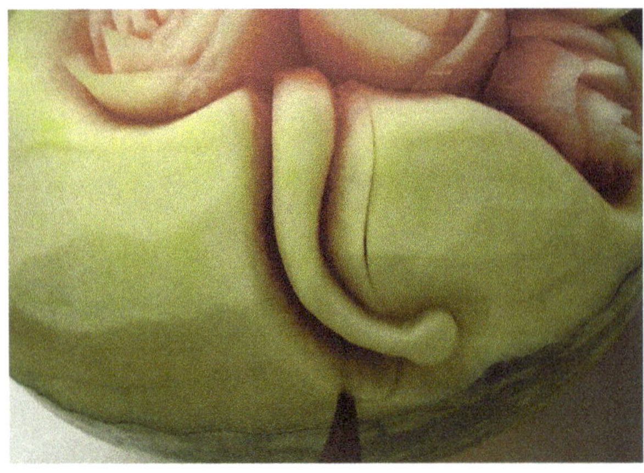

Step 43 – Start to draw the petal of the Lily Flower under the cone that you earlier did.

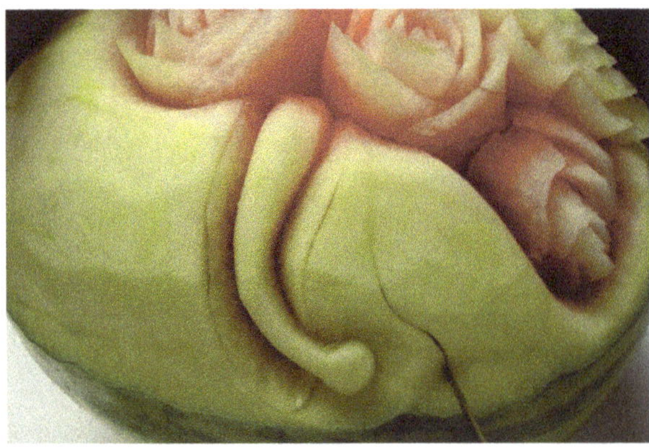

Step 44 – Not so far from the first lily petal, draw the second petal on the right side.

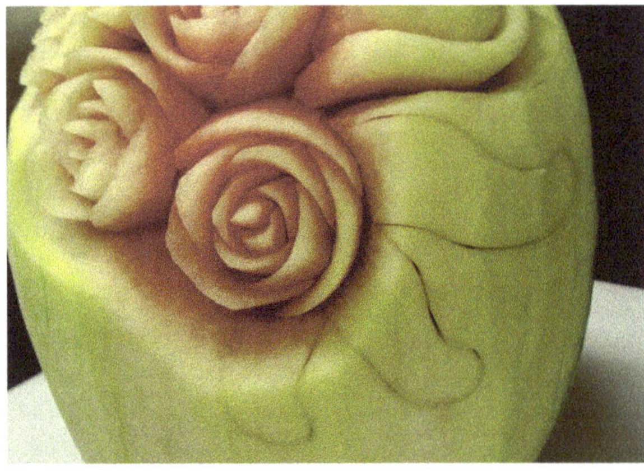

Step 45 – Make three (3) more on the left side.

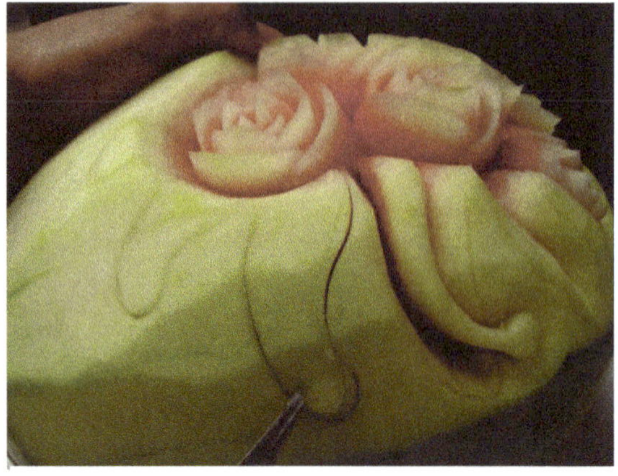

Step 46 – Hold the paring knife at a 60-degree angle then put it in a little deeper as shown in the picture.

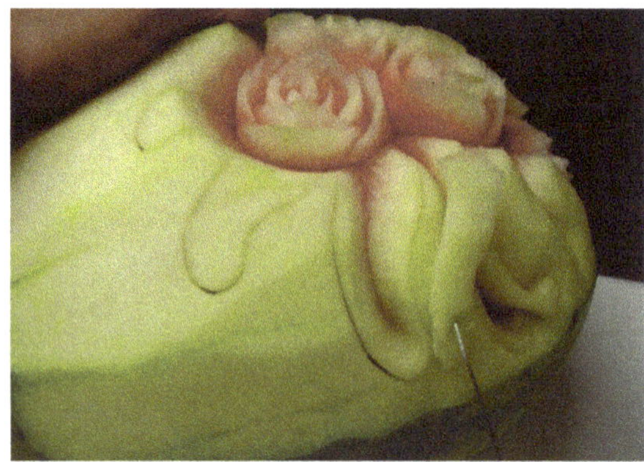

Step 47 – Remove the center portion.

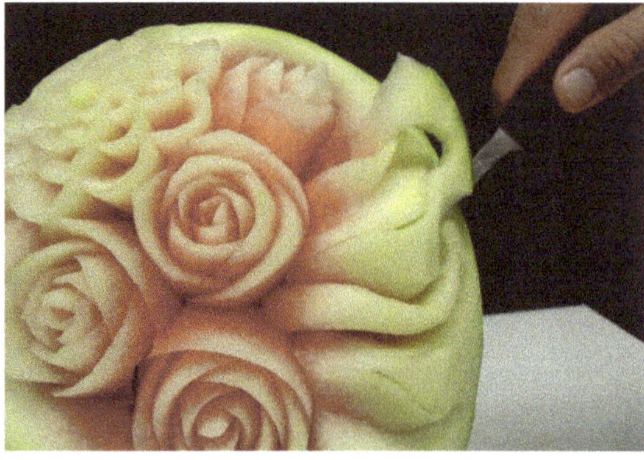

Step 48 – While holding the paring knife at a 60-degree angle, remove all the flesh on the sides of the petals as shown in the picture.

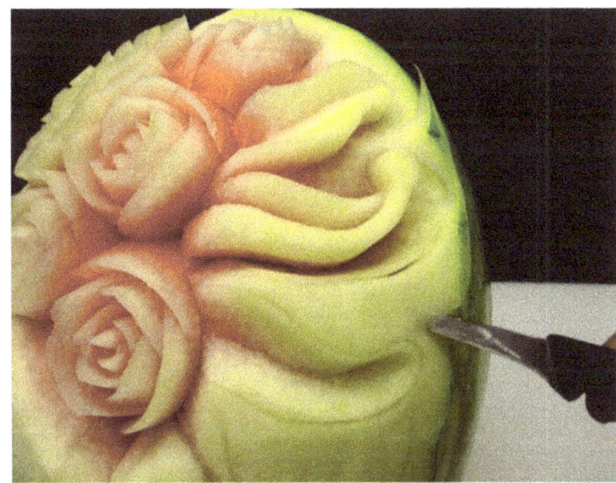

Step 49 – Continue removing the flesh on each side.

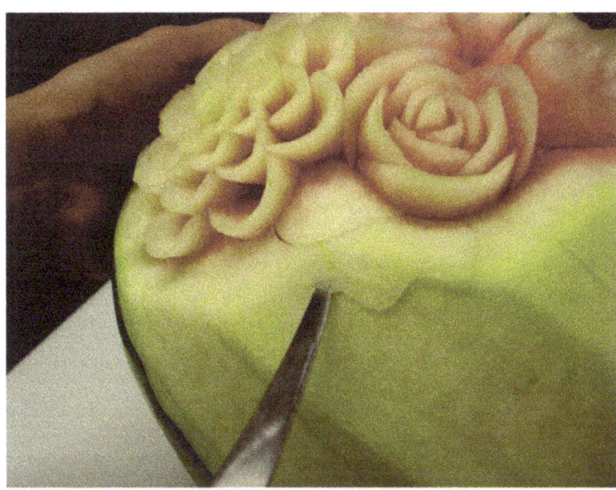

Step 51 – Hold the paring knife at a 45-degree angle then remove the side part as shown in the picture.

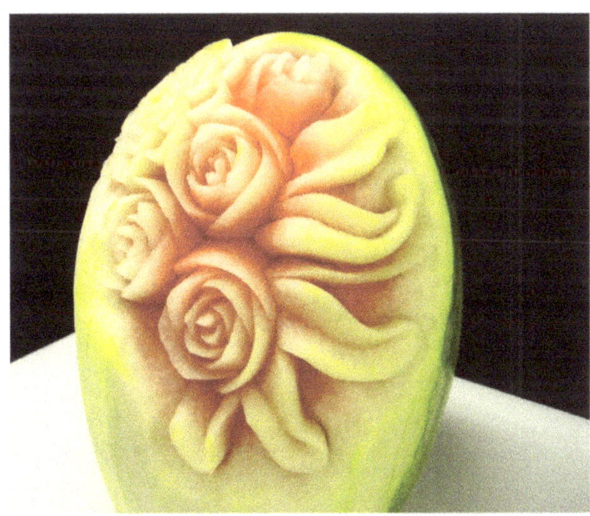

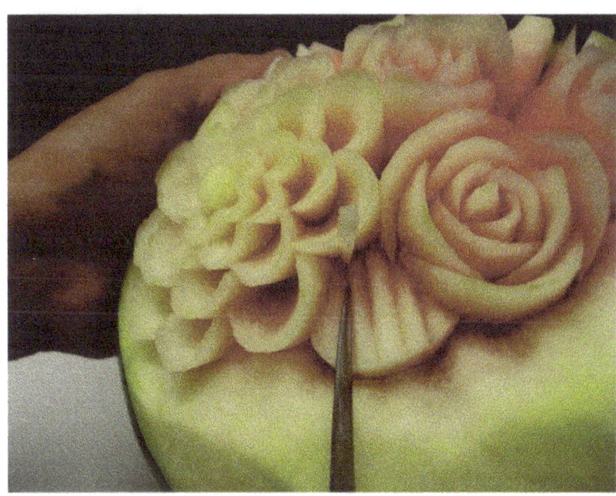

Step 52 – Make vertical lines on top or V-shaped lines.

Step 50 – Hold the paring knife at a 90-degree angle then draw a C-shaped line as shown in the picture.

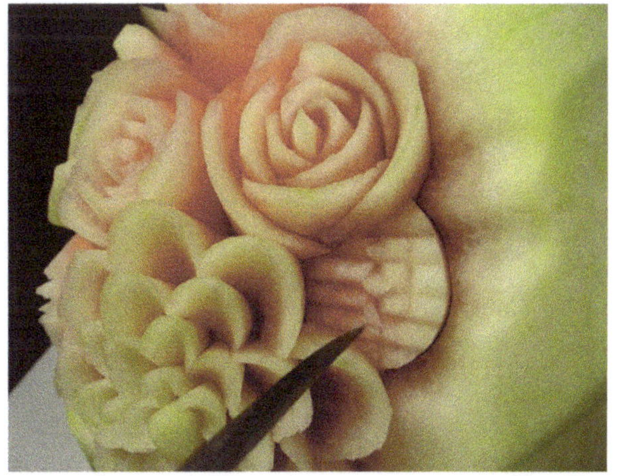

Step 53 – Then make horizontal lines as shown in the picture.

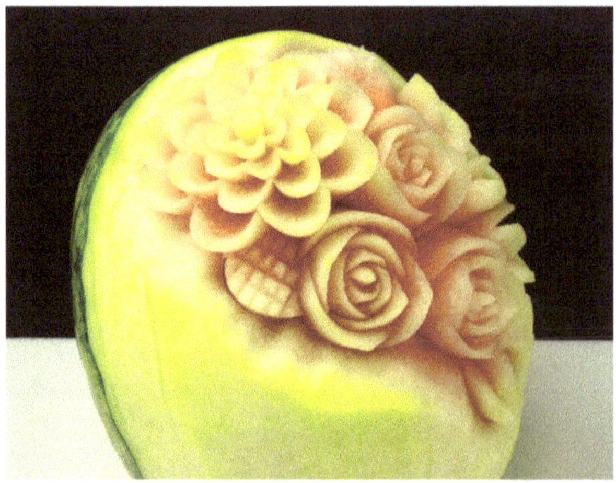

Step 54 – This is the figure on the center of a flower.

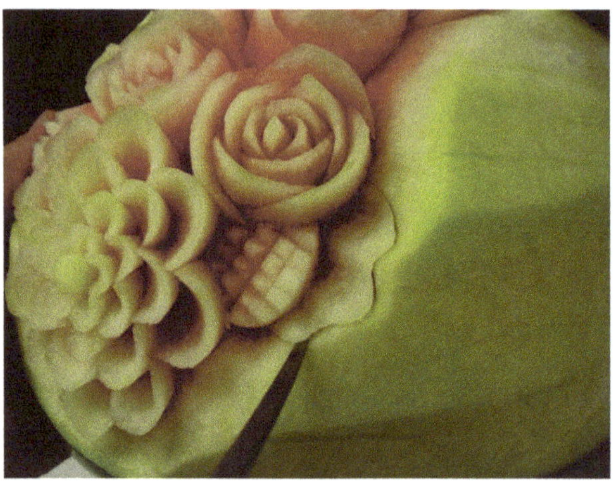

Step 55 – Hold the paring knife at a 65-degree angle then draw the first petal.

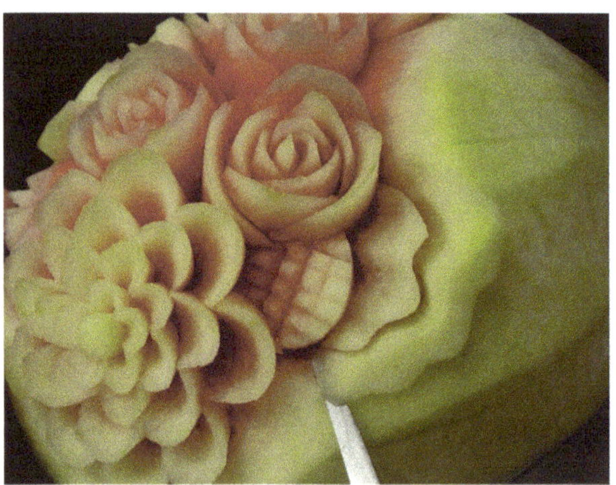

Step 56 – Remove the outer flesh while moving your knife in a wave-like motion.

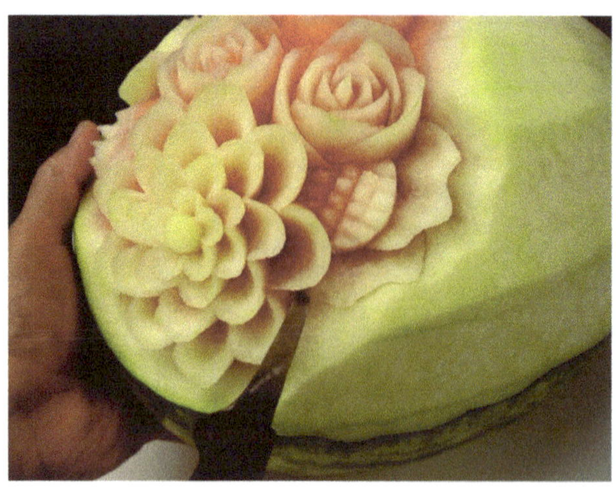

Step 57 – Carve the second petal starting from the middle of the first petal on its left side as shown in the picture.

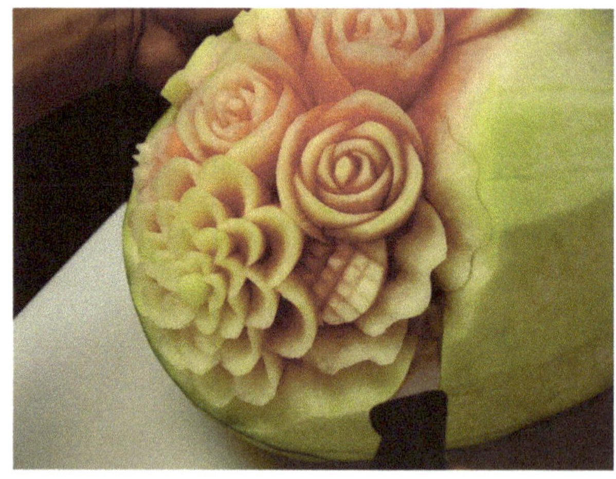

Step 58 – Then carve another petal on the right side of the first petal.

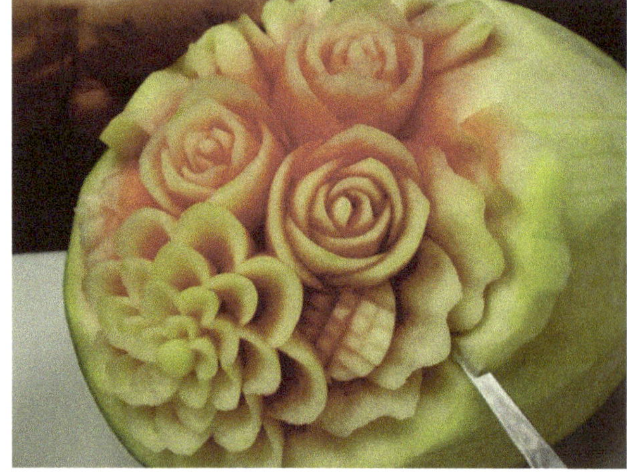

Step 59 – Again, remove the flesh on the outer portion to lift up the shape of the petal.

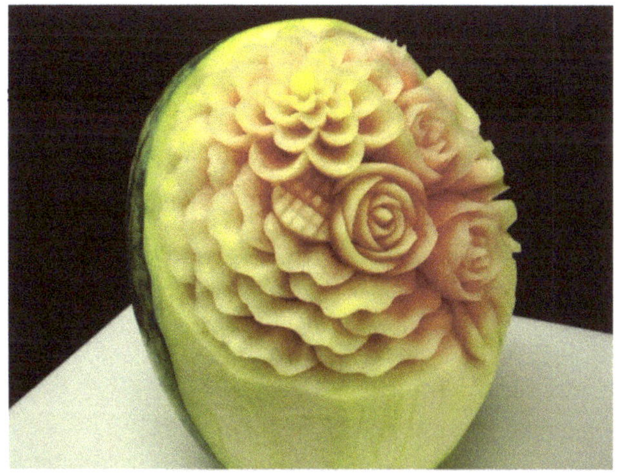

Step 60 – Continue doing the procedure until it looks like the one on this picture.

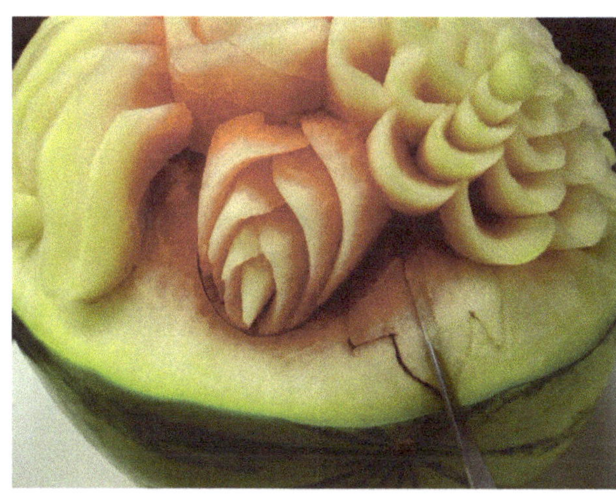

Step 63 – Cut a V-line on the center of the leaf.

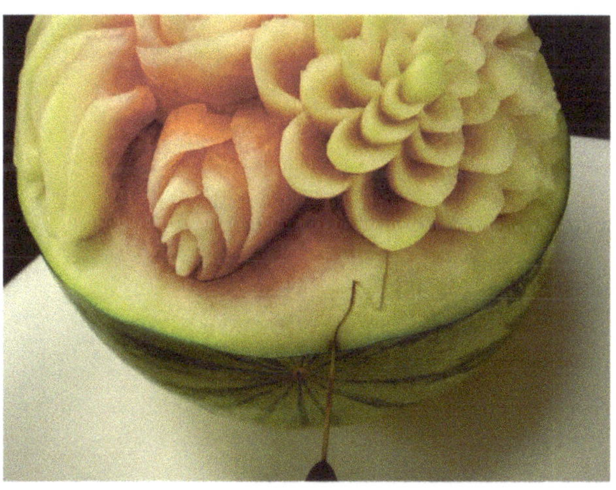

Step 61 – Draw the shape of a leaf on the side of the young rose.

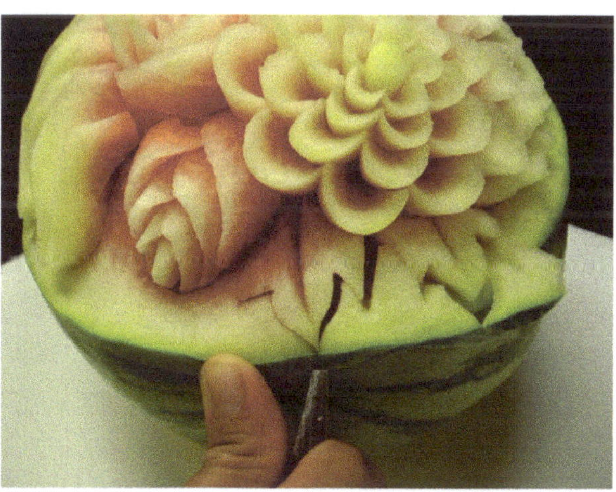

Step 64 – Remove the outer flesh to show the shape of the leaf.

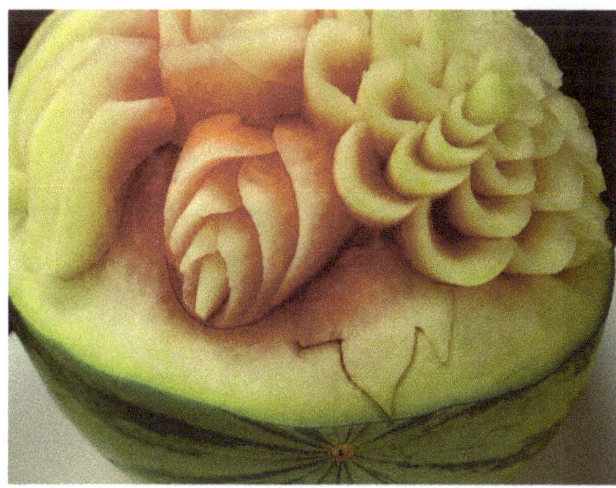

Step 62 – This is how the shape of the leaf looks like.

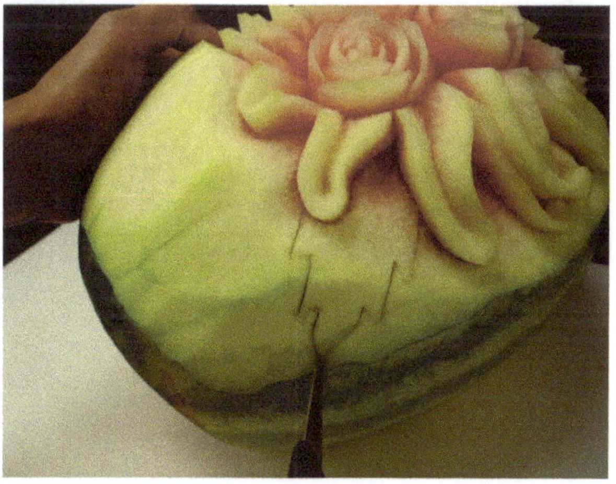

Step 65 – Draw another shape of a leaf at the bottom portion.

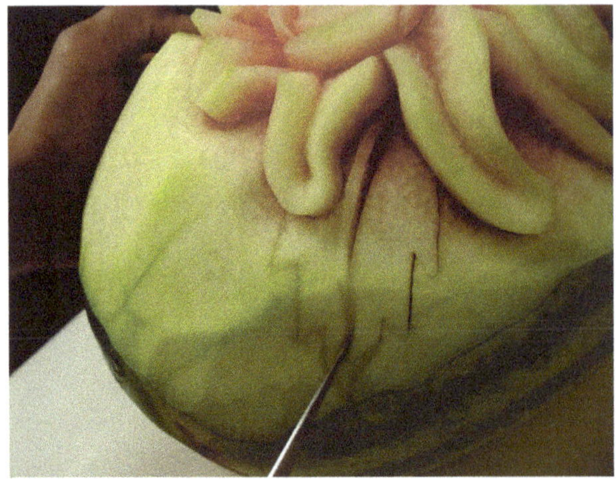

Step 66 – Cut a V-line on the center of the leaf.

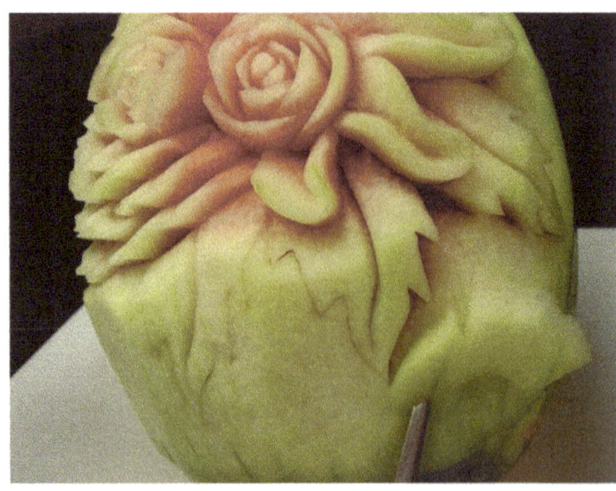

Step 69 – Slowly clean-up the entire surface of the leaves.

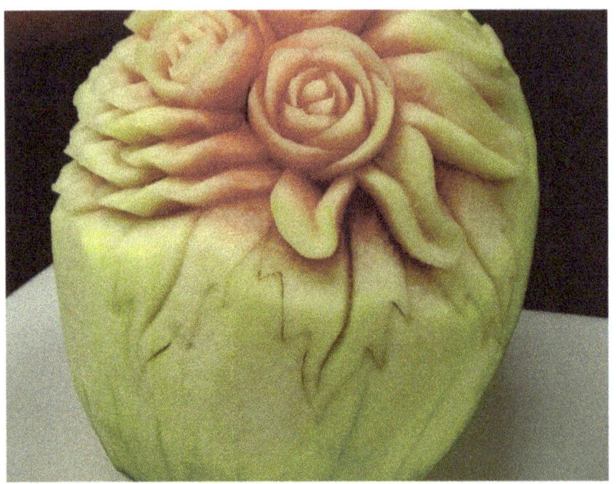

Step 67 – Continue doing the same process.

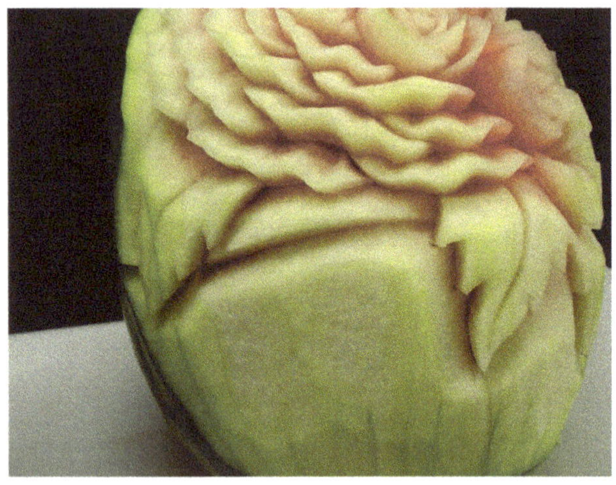

Step 70 – This is how it should look like.

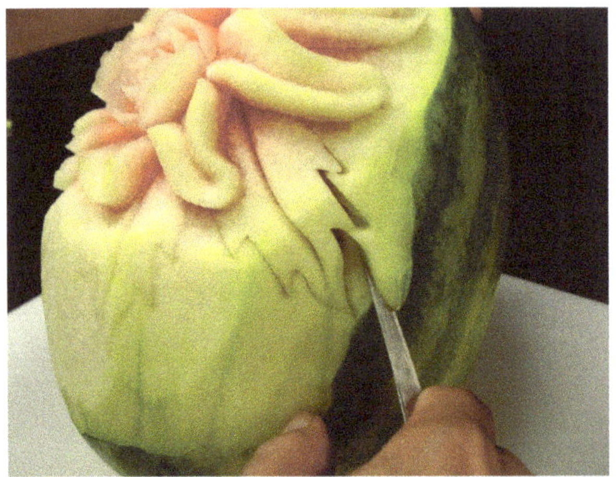

Step 68 – Remove the flesh on the outer side to lift it up.

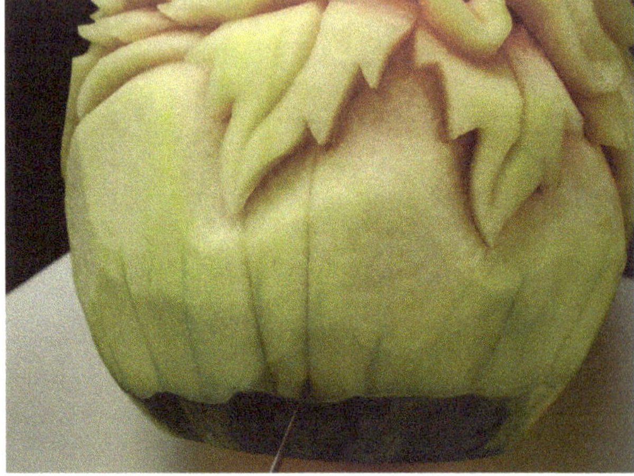

Step 71 – Draw a straight line below the leaves.

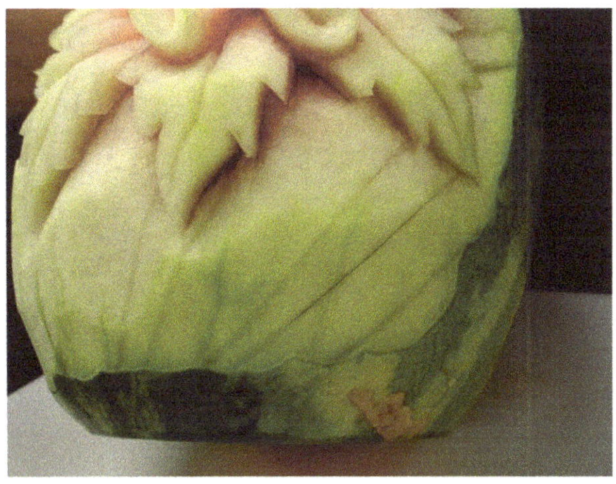

Step 72 – Draw a slanting line starting from the tip of the leaves down to the bottom part as shown in the picture.

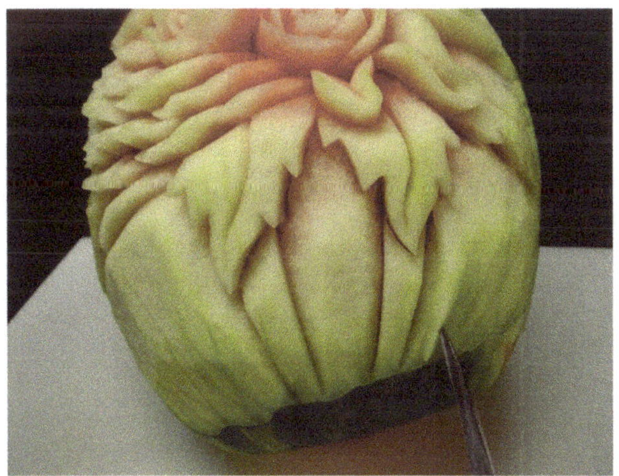

Step 73 – Remove the outer flesh.

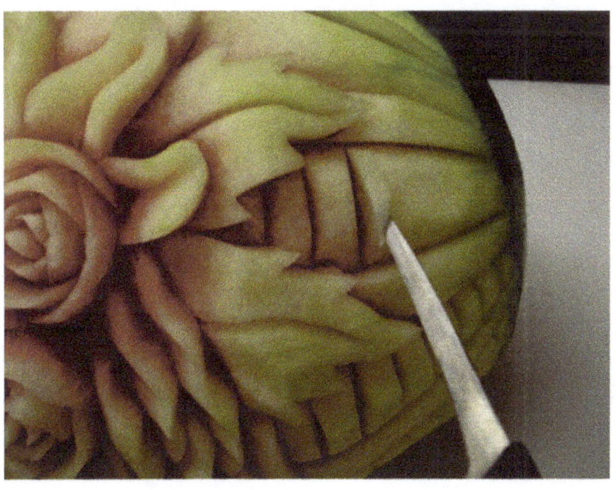

Step 74 – Carve a line in a horizontal way as shown in the picture.

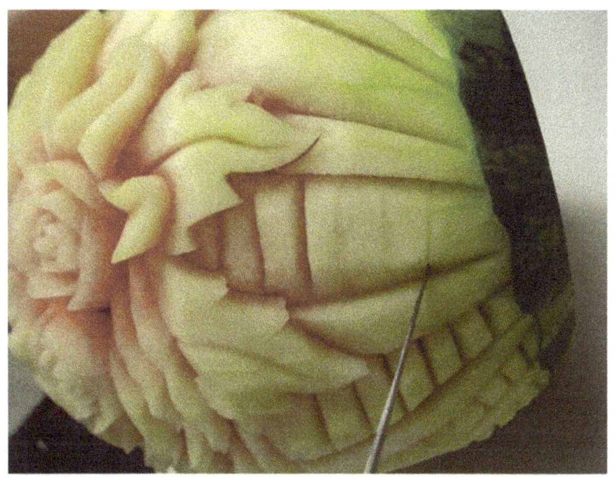

Step 75 – A V-shaped chisel carving tool can be used when doing the shape of a basket.

How to Engrave a Figure in a Basket

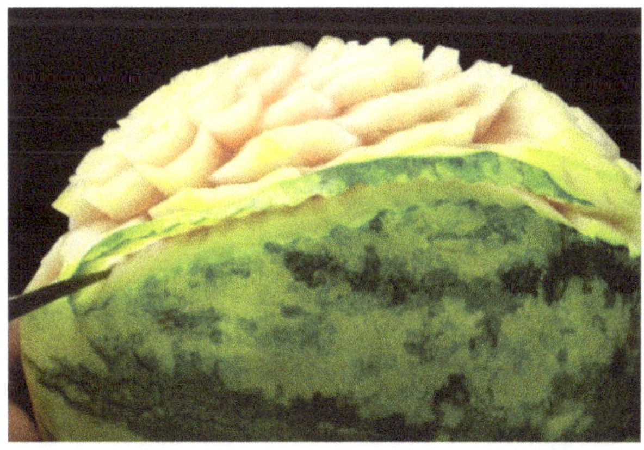

Step 76 – After having done the basket, clean up the sidings all around the figure as shown in the picture

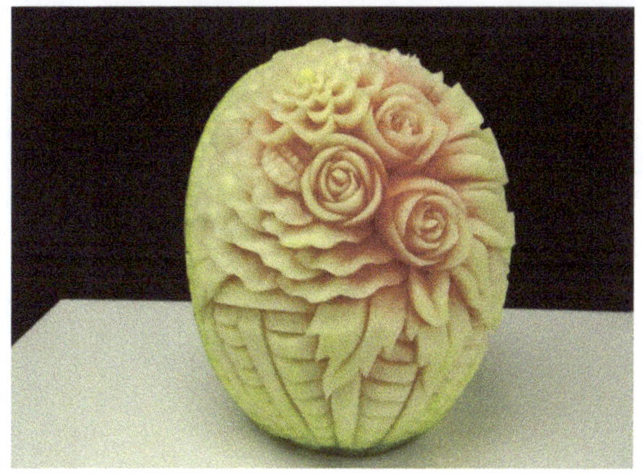

Step 77 – Now this is the complete finished product for the watermelon carving.

Wild Roses

Ice Sculpture

Ice Sculpture

Ice sculpture is a form of sculpture that uses ice as the raw material. Sculpture from ice can be abstract or realistic and can be functional or purely decorative. Ice sculptures are generally associated with special or extravagant events because of their limited lifetime.

The lifetime of a sculpture is determined primarily by the temperature of its environment and thus, sculpture can last from mere minutes to possibly months. There are several ice festivals held around the world, hosting competition of ice carving.

Raw material

Sculpting ice presents a number of difficulties due to the variability and volatility of the material. Ice may be sculpted in a wide range of temperatures and the characteristics of the ice will change according to its temperature as well as the surrounding temperatures. Sculptures are generally carved from blocks free of undesired impurities. Typically, ideal carving is made from pure, clean water. However, clear, transparent ice is a result of the freezing process and not necessarily related to the purity of the water. Clear ice blocks are usually the result of slow freezing from one direction, often with circulation of the water that allows impurities to escape. The water molecules are allowed to line up into the typical crystal lattice while impurities in the unfrozen water. Certain machines and process allow for slow freezing and the removal of impurities and therefore are able to produce the clear blocks of the ice that are favored by ice carvers. However, not all block that are carved are clear ice. White ice blocks look like snow and are sometimes carve. Colored ice blocks are produce by adding dyes to the ice and can be carve as well. In some instances, clear ice colored ice is combined to create to desired effect.

About Ice Carving

The technic started with simple tools such as flat chisel with 3 inches width and flat chisel with 1 ½ inches width, and V-shape chisel progressed to electric chain saw, torches and clamp.

Ice for carving is available in blocks. The standard sizes is 300 lbs. (135 kg.) the dimensions are 40"x 20"x 10 (1m x 50cm x 25 cm.) and the melting ratio: 1 ½ "(38mm) per hour at room temperature.

Techniques

The temperature of the environment affects how quickly the piece must be completed to avoid the effects of melting; if the sculpting does not take place in a cold environment, then the sculptor must work quickly to finish his piece. Some sculpture can be completed in as little as 40 minutes if the carver is using power tools such as chainsaws and special bits fitted to a die grinder. Ice sculpture also use razor-sharp chisel and hand saws that are specifically design for cutting ice.

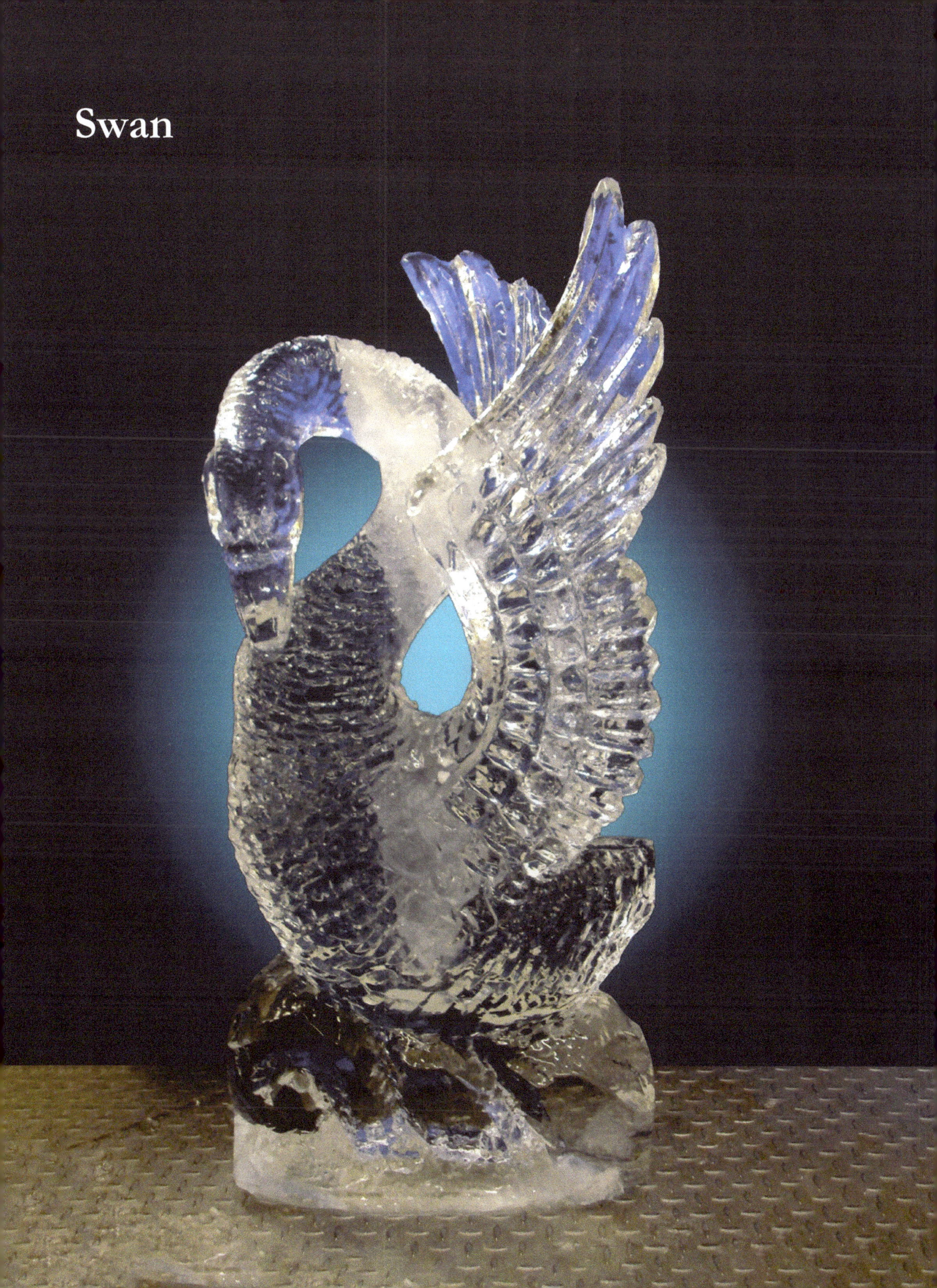
Swan

Love Birds

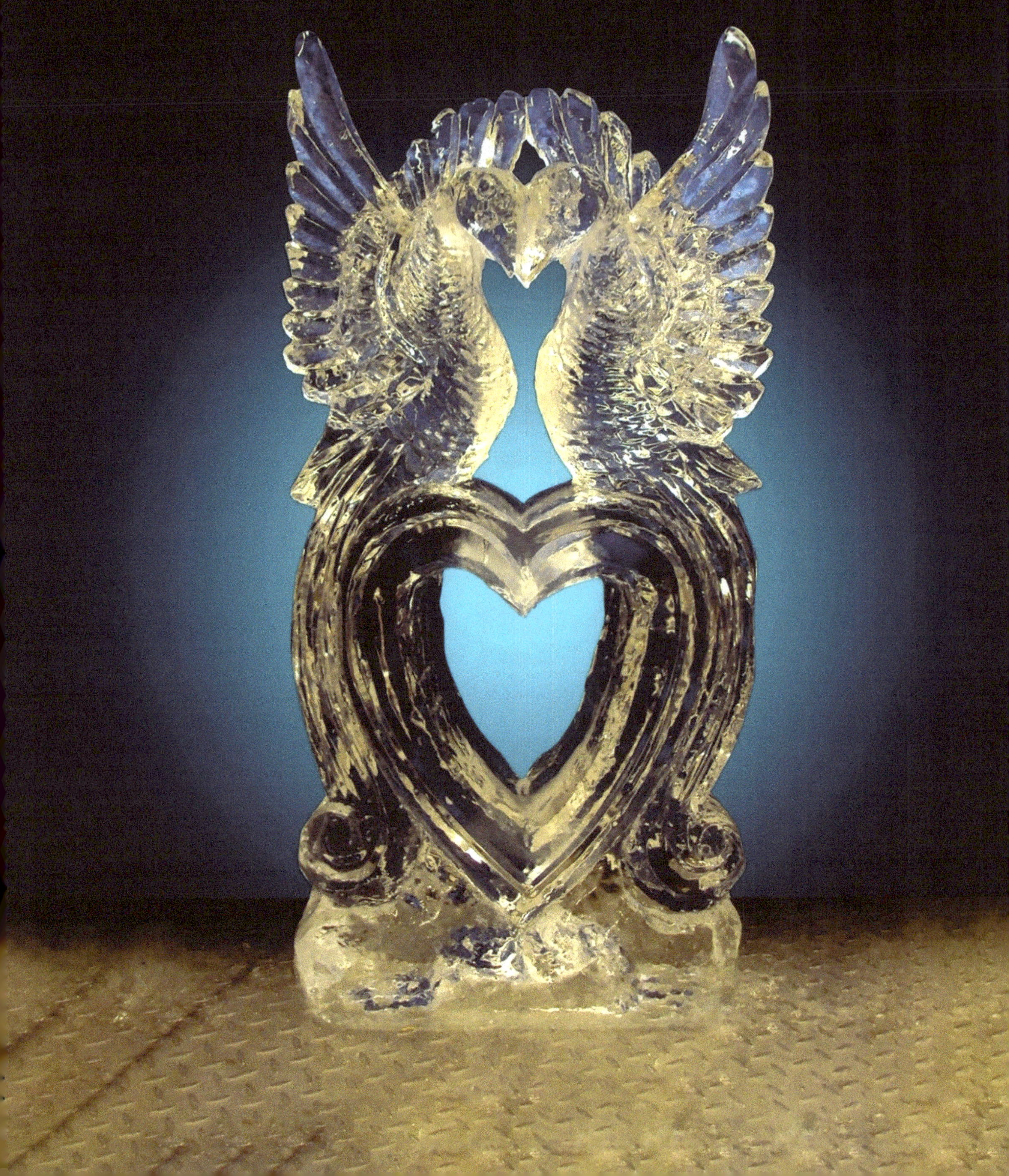

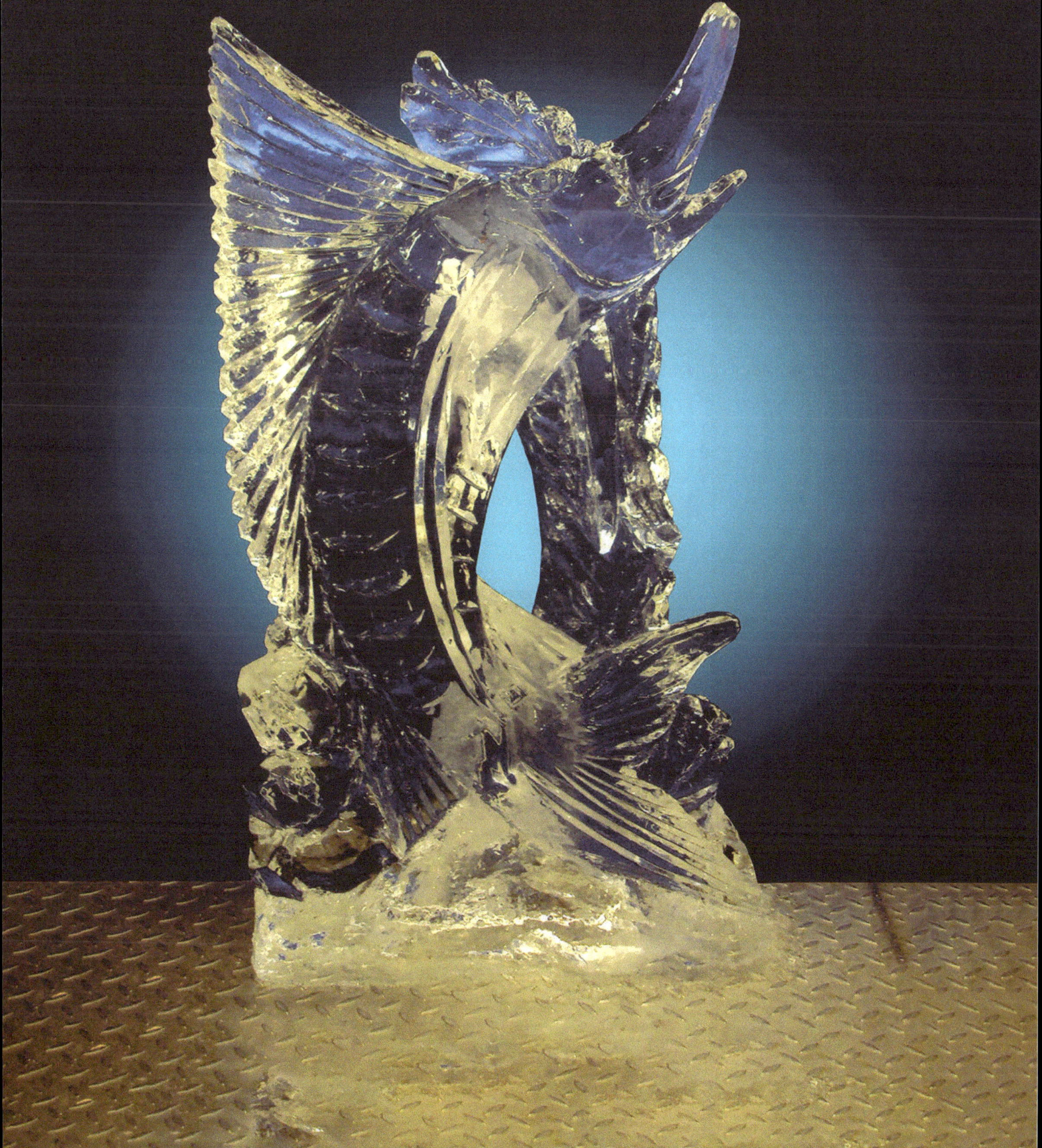

Dolphin

Santa Claus

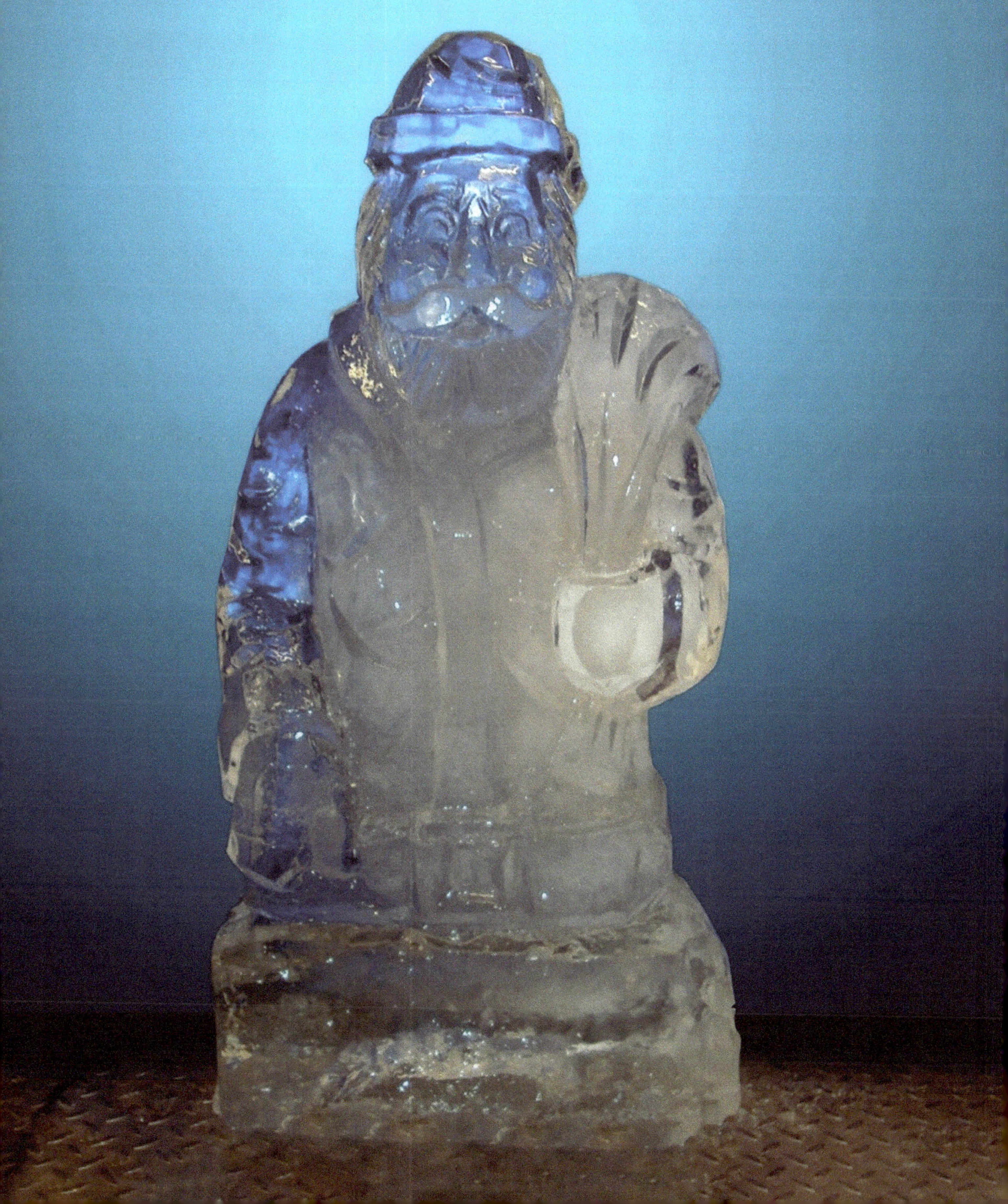

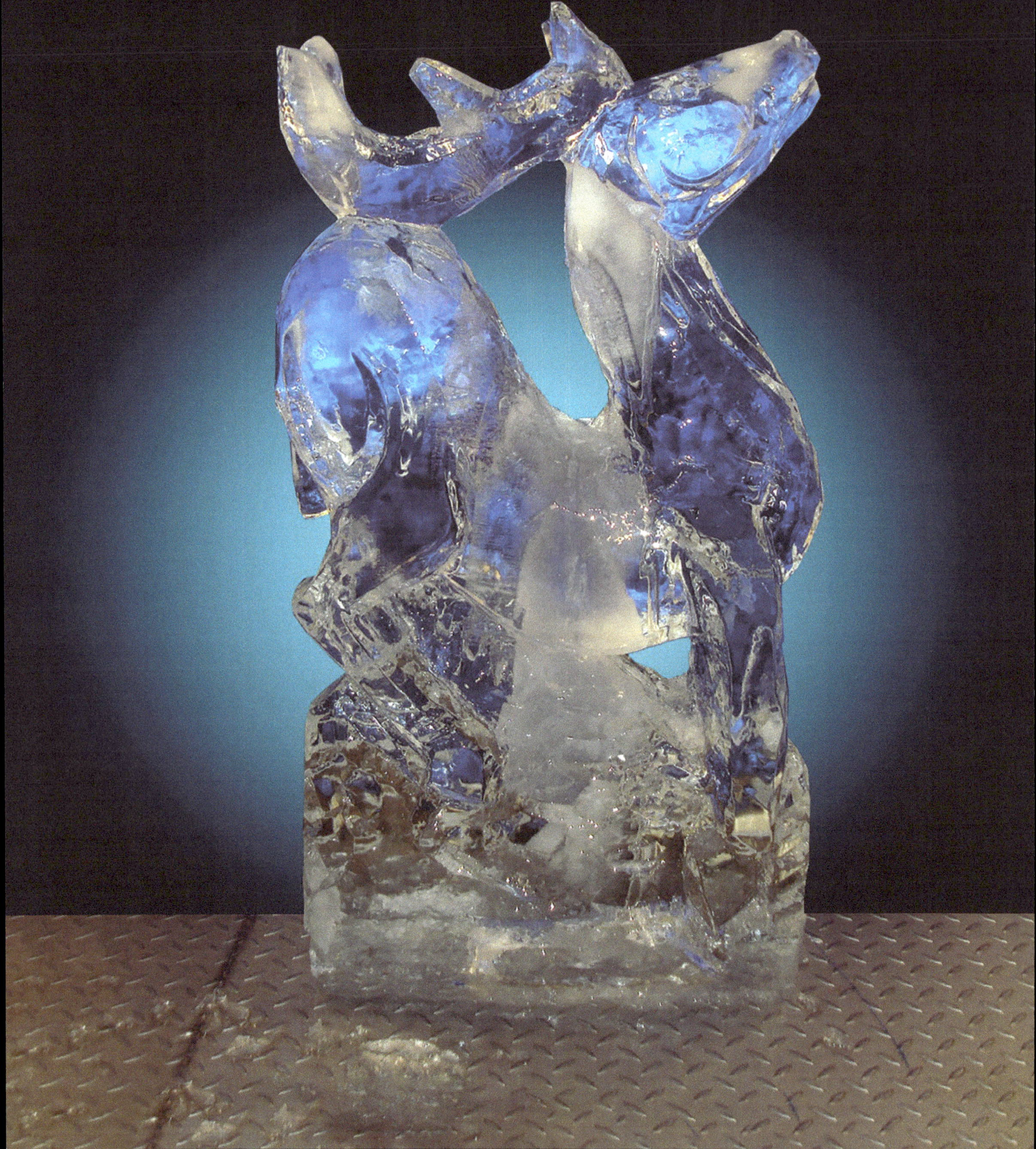

Ram

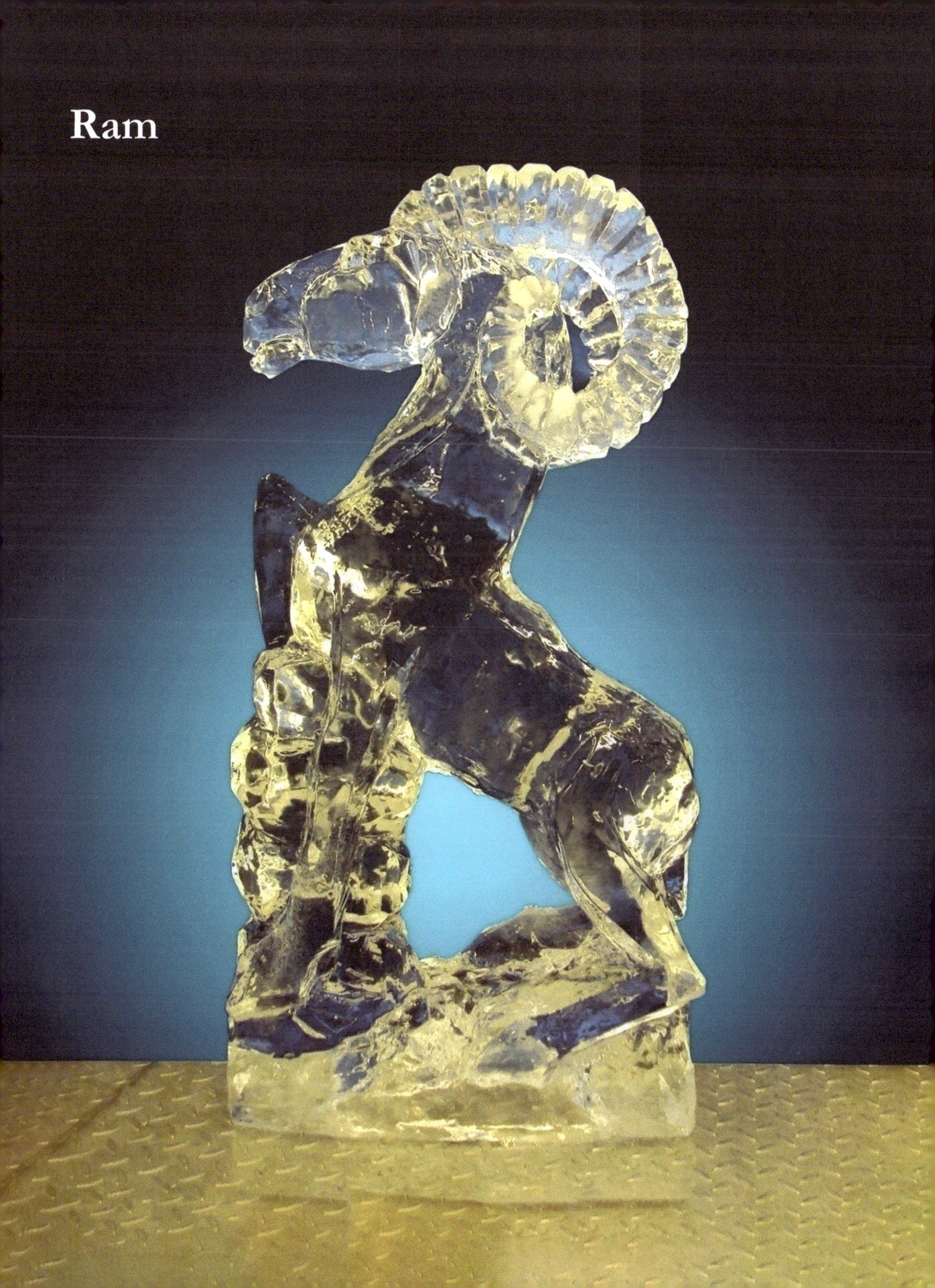

Tallow-wax
Butter Carving

Tallow-wax Butter Carving

History of Tallow Carving

Sculpting tallow goes back to 300 years ago wherein during the early days of the 17th century; the chefs would sculpt butter into provocative shapes for the visual enjoyment of their patrons. Imagine the difficulty of this task without the convenience of refrigeration! In an effort to make life easier, chefs from Europe began to combine butter with animal fats and later on with wax to create a stabilized and creamy sculpting medium that was easier to work with and had a very much longer shelf life.

Modern Tallow

The modern tallow, when worked by hand, quickly softens. It can be formed to take on any shape or built up on any support structure to create sculptures of amazing size and complexity. Modern tallow can be trimmed with tools and knives can add to or remove from until perfection is achieved.

Casting Tallow

This is extremely firm tallow that cannot be softened by hand and on a large-scale basis, requires a great effort to carve on. This is melted and poured into a mould to produce the final sculpture. The hardness of this tallow is ideal because removing if from the mould, especially for one piece rubber moulds, is sometimes a rigorous process.

Different Kinds of Tallow

White Tallow - A blend of purified beef fat and highly refined food grade waxes to create ivory colored tallow with an indefinite shelf life.

Chocolate Tallow – Real chocolate is blended with tallow to create a stable, non-blooming sculpting medium with the color, fragrance and shine of chocolate.

Butter Tallow – Natural butter coloring agents are added to the tallow to give it the look of real butter.

Cheddar Tallow – Looks like real cheddar cheese! The same natural coloring agents that are added to cheddar cheese are incorporated into this tallow.

Sea Creatures

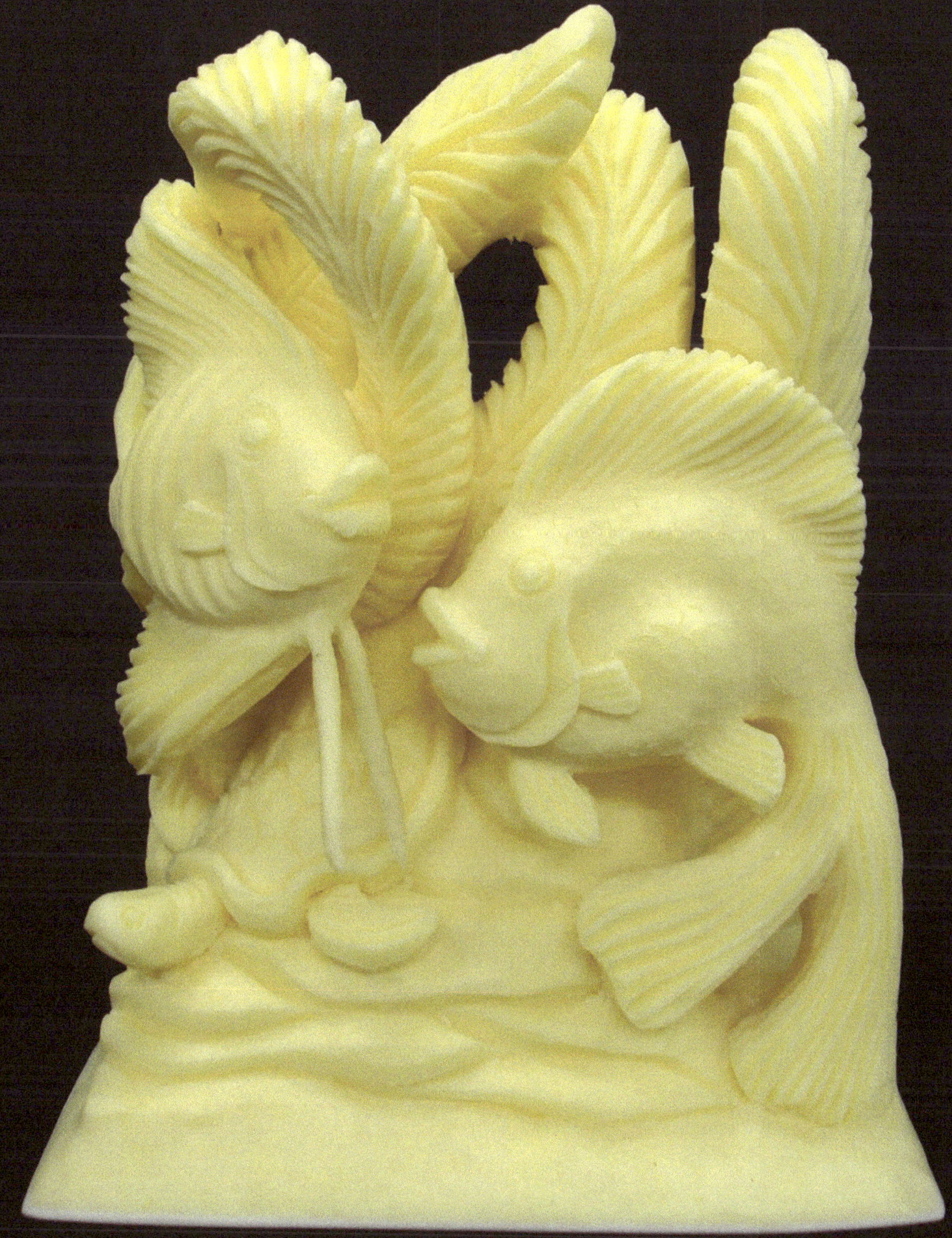

Japanese - Geisha

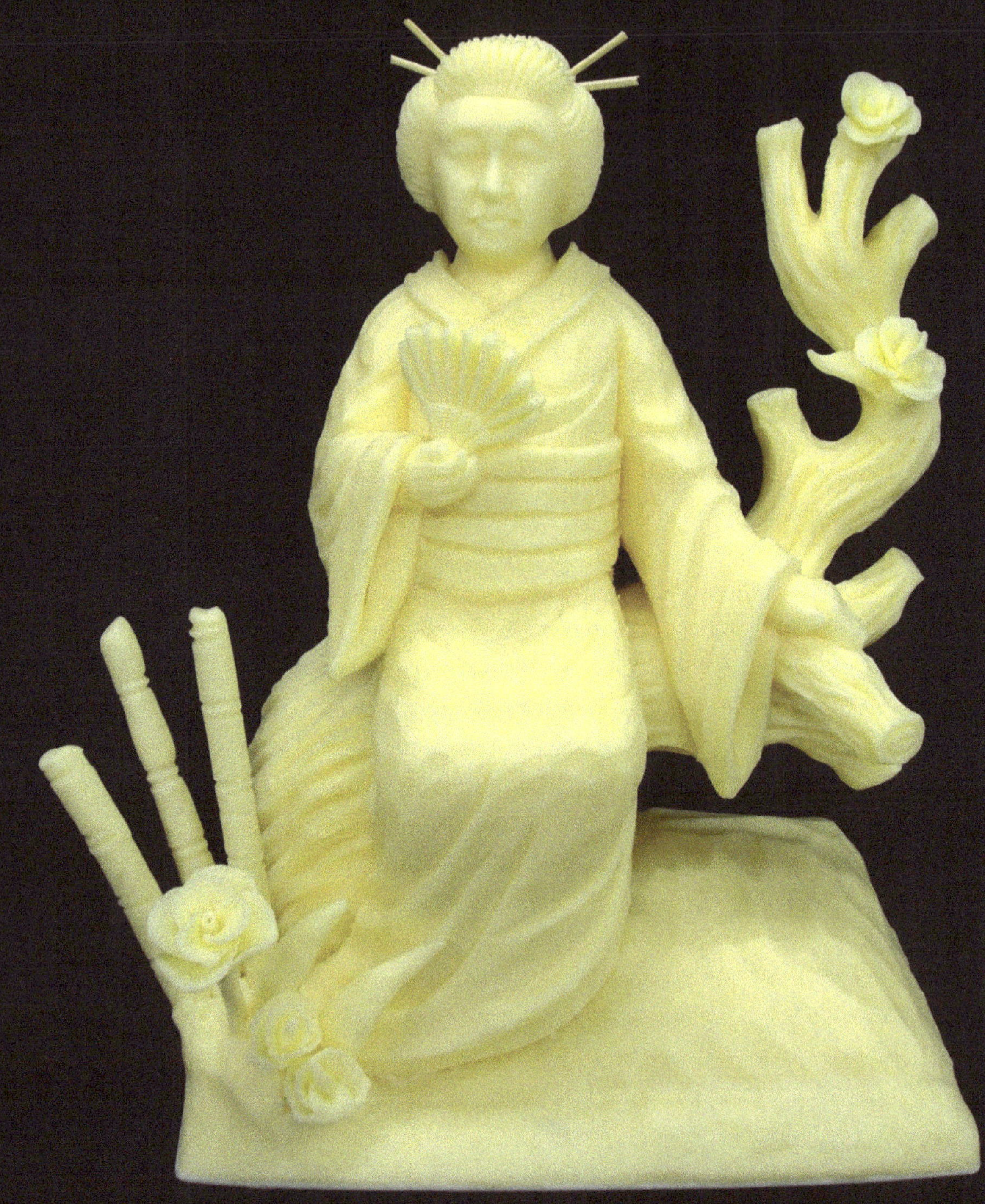

Duck

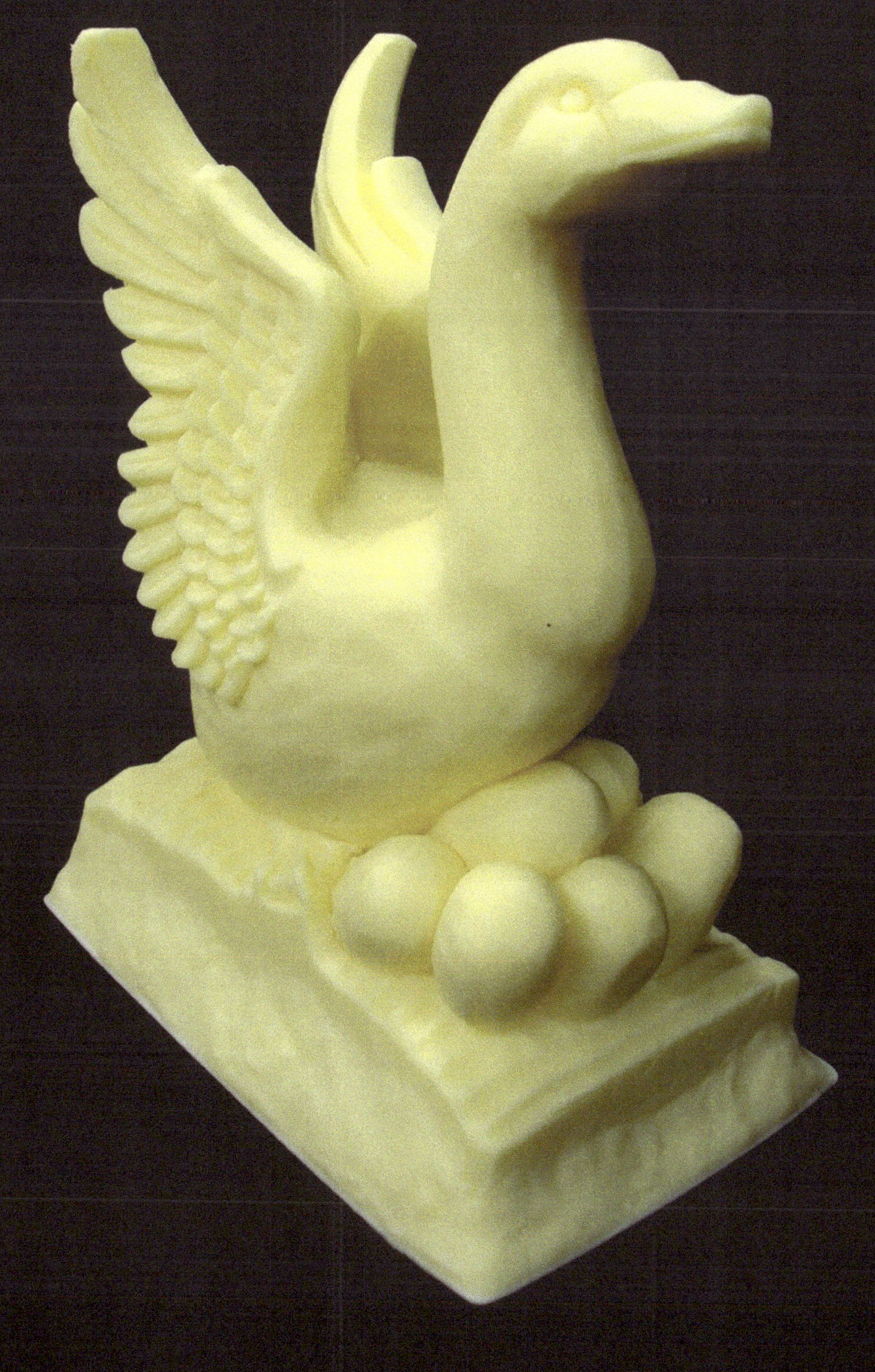

Blue Marlin

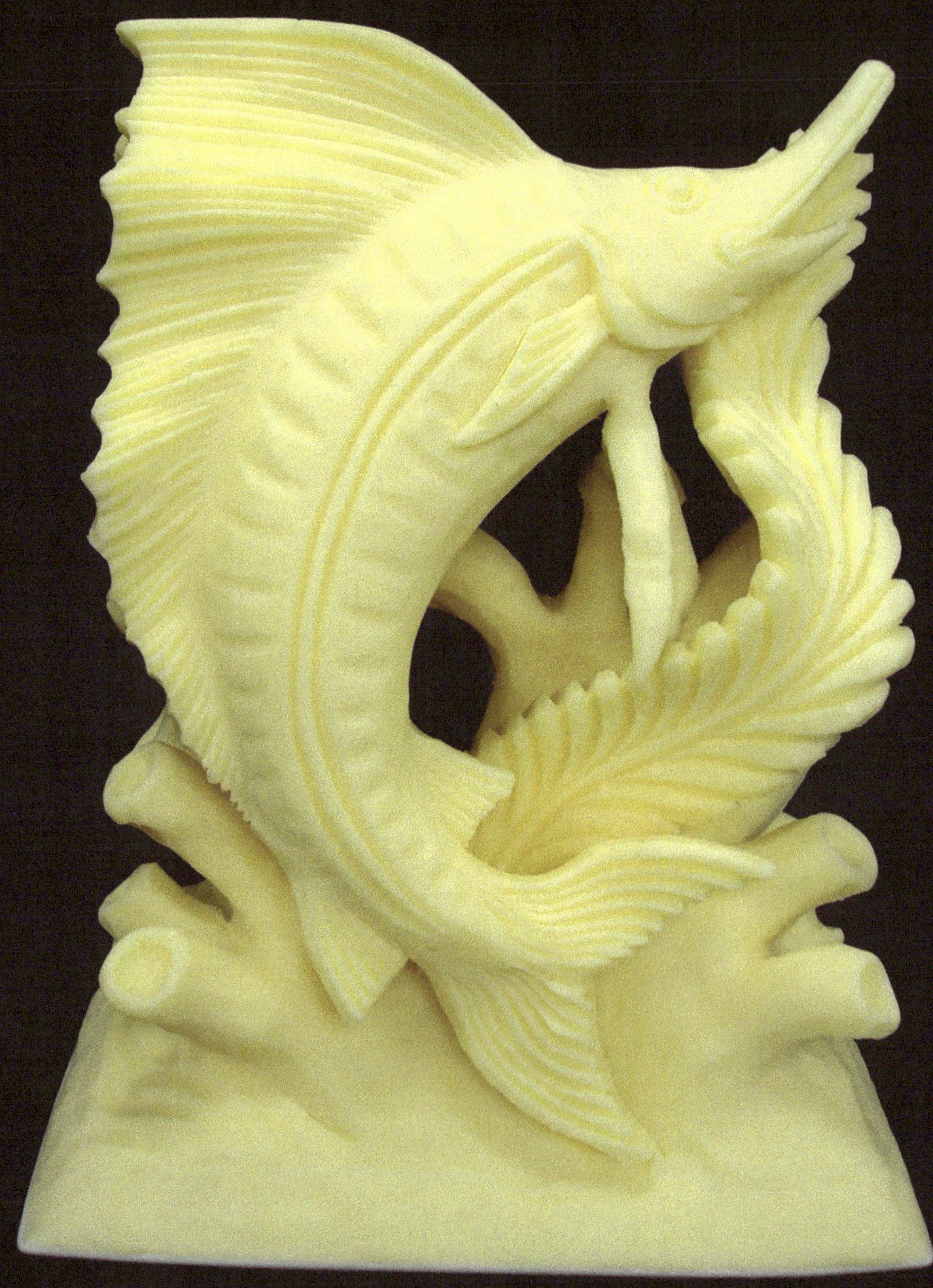

Fruit and Vegetable Carving Book

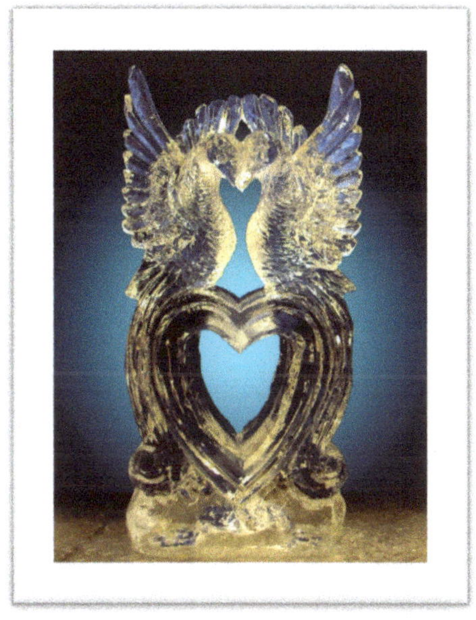

- Want to create stunning table centerpieces design?
- Create impressive food decoration?
- Put extraordinary design to your cuisine?

This book is intended to give step-by-step instruction and techniques in food carving.

Easy to follow steps making the complex design to be simple to execute.

This book is as excellent resource for practical manual of self-study in culinary world.

Book Inside:

- Ice Sculpture
- Tallow-wax Butter Sculpture
- Watermelon Carving
- Vegetable Animation
- Vegetable Flower Bouquet

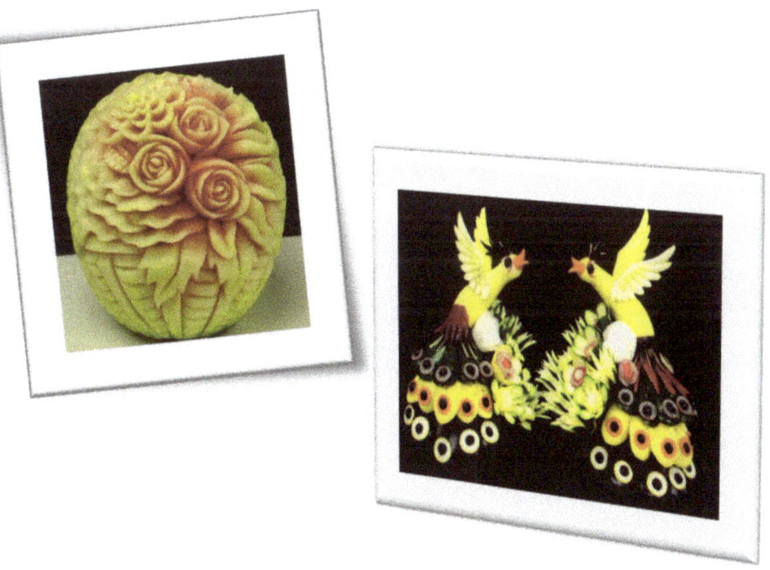

We served in a product of years of experience from famous Luxury Cruise Line around the world.